Better Homes and Gardens®

Hometown
FAVORITES

Delicious down-home recipes

Volume 6

Meredith Consumer Marketing
Des Moines, Iowa

Better Homes and Gardens®

Hometown Favorites

MEREDITH CONSUMER MARKETING
Vice President, Consumer Marketing: Janet Donnelly
Consumer Marketing Product Director: Heather Sorensen
Consumer Marketing Product Manager: Wendy Merical
Business Director: Ron Clingman
Senior Production Manager: Al Rodruck

WATERBURY PUBLICATIONS, INC.
Editorial Director: Lisa Kingsley
Associate Editor: Tricia Bergman
Creative Director: Ken Carlson
Associate Design Director: Doug Samuelson
Contributing Art Director: Mindy Samuelson
Contributing Writer: Lisa Kingsley
Contributing Copy Editors: Gretchen Kauffman, Peg Smith
Contributing Indexer: Elizabeth T. Parson

BETTER HOMES AND GARDENS® MAGAZINE
Editor in Chief: Gayle Goodson Butler
Deputy Editor, Food and Entertaining: Nancy Wall Hopkins

MEREDITH NATIONAL MEDIA GROUP
President: Tom Harty

MEREDITH CORPORATION
Chairman and Chief Executive Officer: Stephen M. Lacy

In Memoriam: E.T. Meredith III (1933–2003)

Better Homes and Gardens®

Test Kitchen

Our seal assures you that every recipe in *Hometown Favorites* has been tested in the Better Homes and Gardens® Test Kitchen. This means that each recipe is practical and reliable, and meets our high standards of taste appeal. We guarantee your satisfaction with this book for as long as you own it.

All of us at Meredith Consumer Marketing are dedicated to providing you with information and ideas to enhance your home. We welcome your comments and suggestions. Write to us at: Meredith Consumer Marketing, 1716 Locust St., Des Moines, IA 50309-3023.

Pictured on front cover:
Four-Layer Caramel Crunch Nougat Brownies, page 171

Contents

CHAPTER 1

Appetizers

These savory nibbles and bites can be a prelude to dinner—or a generous spread of them can be dinner. For perfect-party planning, look no further.

9

17

29

Spicy Apple-Glazed Meatballs

Everybody loves a meatball and a cocktail fork to spear it with. These beef meatballs are made sweet with brown sugar and apple juice and spicy with cayenne pepper.

PREP 20 minutes
STAND 10 minutes
COOK 12 minutes

12 servings	ingredients	24 servings
1	egg	2
¼ cup	milk	½ cup
2 slices	white or whole wheat bread, torn	4 slices
1 lb.	85% lean ground beef	2 lb.
4 cloves	garlic, minced	8 cloves
½ tsp.	freshly ground black pepper	1 tsp.
¼ tsp.	salt	½ tsp.
¼ tsp.	cayenne pepper	½ tsp.
1 Tbsp.	vegetable oil	2 Tbsp.
1 cup	apple juice or pear nectar	2 cups
¼ cup	reduced-sodium soy sauce	½ cup
3 Tbsp.	packed brown sugar	6 Tbsp.
1½ tsp.	cornstarch	3 tsp.
1 tsp.	ground ginger	2 tsp.
¼ tsp.	cayenne pepper	½ tsp.
6	green onions, chopped	12

1. For the spicy meatballs, in a large bowl whisk together egg and milk. Add bread. Let stand 10 minutes, just until bread is softened. Add beef, garlic, black pepper, salt, and cayenne pepper. Mix thoroughly with hands or wooden spoon. For 12 servings, shape into 48 meatballs.

2. In an extra-large skillet heat oil over medium heat. Cook meatballs, half at a time, about 6 minutes per batch, turning occasionally until brown and crusty on outside and no longer pink inside. Transfer meatballs to a covered dish; cover to keep warm. Drain fat from skillet; wipe out skillet.

3. For the apple glaze, in a small bowl combine apple juice, soy sauce, brown sugar, cornstarch, ginger, and cayenne pepper. In the same skillet the meatballs were cooked cook and stir juice mixture until thickened and bubbly (at full boil). Cook and stir 2 minutes more. Return meatballs to skillet to heat through and coat with sauce. Transfer glazed meatballs a serving dish. Top with green onions.

FOR 24 SERVINGS Prepare using method above, except in Step 1 shape meat mixture into 96 meatballs.

PER SERVING *143 cal., 8 g fat (3 g sat. fat), 42 mg chol., 297 mg sodium, 10 g carb., 0 g fiber, 9 g pro.*

Mexican-Style Meatballs and Smokies

This is what to make when you can't decide between sausages and meatballs. Shaping the meatballs with wet hands prevents the mixture from sticking.

1. Preheat oven to 350°F. In a medium bowl combine egg, bread crumbs, onion, snipped cilantro, garlic, and salt. Add ground beef and sausage; mix well. For 12 servings, with wet hands shape into 24 meatballs.

2. Place meatballs in a 15×10×1-inch baking pan. Bake about 15 minutes or until no longer pink (160°F). Drain off fat.

3. In a large saucepan stir together salsa and chili sauce. Stir in baked meatballs and sausage links. Cook over medium-high heat until heated through, stirring occasionally.

4. Serve immediately or keep warm, covered, in a 3½- or 4-quart slow cooker on warm setting or low-heat setting up to 2 hours. Use skewers, toothpicks, or a slotted spoon to serve meatballs and sausages. If desired, garnish with cilantro sprigs.

FOR 24 SERVINGS Prepare using method above, except in Step 1 shape meat mixture into 48 meatballs.

PER SERVING *148 cal., 11 g fat (4 g sat. fat), 34 mg chol., 648 mg sodium, 6 g carb., 1 g fiber, 7 g pro.*

PREP 30 minutes
BAKE 15 minutes at 350°F

12 servings	ingredients	24 servings
1	egg, lightly beaten	1
3 Tbsp.	fine dry bread crumbs	¼ cup
2 Tbsp.	finely chopped onion	¼ cup
1 Tbsp.	snipped fresh cilantro	2 Tbsp.
1 clove	garlic, minced	3 cloves
¼ tsp.	salt	½ tsp.
4 oz.	lean ground beef	8 oz.
4 oz.	uncooked chorizo sausage (casing removed if necessary)	8 oz.
½	16-oz. jar salsa	1
½	12-oz. jar chili sauce	1
½	16-oz. pkg. small cooked smoked sausage links	1
	Fresh cilantro sprigs (optional)	

Maple-Mustard Sausages

Pure maple syrup and freshly snipped sage intensify the flavorings in these breakfast-sausages-turned-cocktail snack.

1. In a large skillet cook sausages according to package directions. Drain fat from skillet.

2. Meanwhile, in a small bowl stir together brown sugar, maple syrup, mustard, and sage; add to skillet with sausages. Cook, uncovered, over medium heat for 3 to 4 minutes or until sausages are glazed, stirring frequently. Serve immediately.

TO MAKE AHEAD In a small bowl combine brown sugar, maple syrup, mustard, and sage. Cover and chill for up to 24 hours. Prepare as directed.

PER SERVING *343 cal., 24 g fat (8 g sat. fat), 71 mg chol., 685 mg sodium, 13 g carb., 0 g fiber, 17 g pro.*

START TO FINISH **25 minutes**

8 servings	ingredients	16 servings
2	12-oz. pkg. breakfast sausage links	4
¼ cup	packed brown sugar	½ cup
¼ cup	pure maple syrup	½ cup
1 Tbsp.	stone-ground mustard	2 Tbsp.
2 tsp.	snipped fresh sage	4 tsp.

Mojo Chicken Drummies with Cilantro-Mango Sauce

PREP 20 minutes
MARINATE 2 hours
BAKE 25 minutes at 450°F

12 servings	ingredients	24 servings
12 (2 lb.)	chicken wings	24 (4 lb.)
1 cup	mango nectar	2 cups
½ cup	lemon juice	1 cup
½ cup	orange juice	1 cup
½ cup	snipped fresh parsley	1 cup
¼ cup	red wine vinegar	½ cup
¼ cup	olive oil	½ cup
1 to 2	fresh jalapeños, seeded and finely chopped*	2 to 4
6 cloves	garlic, minced	12 cloves
1 tsp.	salt	2 tsp.
½ tsp.	ground cumin	1 tsp.
1	mango, seeded, peeled, and chopped	2
⅓ cup	chopped onion	⅔ cup
	Orange slices (optional)	
	Fresh cilantro sprigs	

To prepare the mango, cut down the side of the fruit on either side of the large seed. Score the flesh in each half in a crosshatch pattern, then run a long, thin knife underneath the flesh to separate it from the skin.

1. Cut off and discard tips of chicken wings or reserve for making broth. Cut wings at joints to make 24 pieces. Place chicken in a resealable plastic bag set in a shallow dish.

2. For marinade, in a medium bowl whisk together mango nectar, lemon juice, orange juice, parsley, vinegar, oil, jalapeño, garlic, salt, and cumin. Remove ½ cup of the marinade for sauce; cover and chill until needed.

3. Pour the remaining marinade over chicken. Seal bag; turn to coat chicken. Marinate in the refrigerator for 2 to 24 hours, turning bag occasionally.

4. Preheat oven to 450°F. Drain chicken, discarding marinade. Arrange chicken in a single layer on the unheated rack of a large broiler pan. Bake for 25 minutes or until chicken is golden brown, turning once.

5. Meanwhile, for sauce, in a blender combine the reserved ½ cup marinade, the mango, onion, and cilantro. Cover and blend until smooth. If desired, arrange chicken on a bed of orange slices. Garnish with fresh cilantro sprigs. Serve chicken with sauce.

*TIP Because chile peppers contain volatile oils that can burn skin and eyes, avoid direct contact with them as much as possible. When working with chile peppers, wear plastic or rubber gloves. If bare hands touch peppers, wash hands and nails well with soap and warm water.

FOR 24 SERVINGS Prepare using method above, except in Step 1 cut wings to make 48 pieces. In Step 2 remove 1 cup of the marinade for the sauce.

PER SERVING *278 cal., 20 g fat (4 g sat. fat), 97 mg chol., 283 mg sodium, 9 g carb., 1 g fiber, 17 g pro.*

Bangkok Chile Wings

These skillet-cooked wings are quick and easy to make—just 15 minutes to get them ready to cook and 25 minutes of cooking time.

1. Cut off and discard tips of chicken wings. For 12 servings, cut wings at joints to form 24 pieces. Sprinkle with kosher salt. In a large skillet heat oil over medium-high heat. Add chicken wings; cook about 10 minutes or until brown on both sides. Drain off fat.

2. For sauce, place cut-up mango in a food processor or blender. Cover and process or blend until smooth. Transfer to a small bowl. Stir in coconut milk, Asian chili sauce, and lime juice. Pour sauce over chicken wings in skillet.

3. Bring to simmering. Cook, covered, for 5 minutes. Cook, uncovered, about 10 minutes more or until chicken is no longer pink and sauce is slightly thickened, stirring occasionally and reducing heat as necessary. Season to taste with salt.

4. Transfer to a serving platter. If desired, garnish with mango and cilantro.

FOR 24 SERVINGS Prepare using method above, except in Step 1 cut wings to form 48 pieces.

PER SERVING *151 cal., 11 g fat (3 g sat. fat), 39 mg chol., 586 mg sodium, 4 g carb., 0 g fiber, 9 g pro.*

PREP 15 minutes
COOK 25 minutes

12 servings	ingredients	24 servings
12 (2½ lb.)	chicken wings	24 (5 lb.)
1 Tbsp.	kosher salt	2 Tbsp.
2 Tbsp.	vegetable oil	4 Tbsp.
1 medium	mango, seeded, peeled, and cut up	2 medium
½	14-oz. can unsweetened light coconut milk	1
1 Tbsp.	Asian chili sauce (Sriracha sauce)	2 Tbsp.
1 Tbsp.	lime juice	2 Tbsp.
	Salt	
	Chopped mango (optional)	
	Snipped fresh cilantro (optional)	

Ranch Deviled Eggs

This platter of deviled eggs is particularly colorful, crunchy, and flavorful. A combination of whole cooked egg whites, roma tomatoes, and jalapeño halves serves as vessels for the filling.

1. For 16 servings, coat a small skillet with 1 teaspoon oil; heat over medium heat. Add peppers to hot skillet; cook about 5 minutes or until lightly charred, turning occasionally. Cool.

2. Halve peppers; remove seeds and membranes. Scoop out tomato halves. Set halves aside.

3. For filling, remove yolks from eggs and place in a medium bowl. Add half the egg white halves to bowl; mash with a fork. Stir in yogurt, green onions, cilantro, dressing mix, and 3 tablespoons oil. Spoon filling into halved chile peppers, tomatoes, and remaining egg white halves.

4. Cover and chill for up to 8 hours. If desired, serve with olive slices.

FOR 32 SERVINGS Prepare using method above, except in Step 1 use 2 teaspoons oil and in Step 3 use 6 tablespoons oil.

PER SERVING *90 cal., 6 g fat (2 g sat. fat), 107 mg chol., 192 mg sodium, 3 g carb., 0 g fiber, 5 g pro.*

PREP 30 minutes

16 servings	ingredients	32 servings
1 tsp.	vegetable oil	2 tsp.
4	fresh jalapeños (see tip, page 10)	8
4	roma tomatoes, halved	8
8	hard-cooked eggs, peeled and halved	16
½ cup	plain Greek yogurt	1 cup
¼ cup	thinly sliced green onions	½ cup
2 Tbsp.	snipped fresh cilantro	¼ cup
1	1-oz. pkg. ranch dry salad dressing mix	2
3 Tbsp.	olive oil	6 Tbsp.
4	garlic-stuffed green olives, sliced (optional)	8

Garlicky BBQ Shrimp

These are for the true garlic lovers in your world. Sop up the super flavorful butter with crusty French bread.

1. Thaw shrimp, if frozen. Peel and devein shrimp, leaving tails intact (if desired). Rinse shrimp; pat dry with paper towels.

2. In a large skillet combine oil, butter, garlic, thyme, and bay leaves. Stir over medium heat until butter is melted. In a medium bowl combine sherry, paprika, Worcestershire sauce, and salt. Add shrimp; toss gently to coat. Add coated shrimp to hot butter mixture in skillet. Cook and stir for 3 to 5 minutes or until shrimp are opaque.

3. If desired, transfer shrimp to a serving dish. Remove bay leaves; discard. Serve with lemon wedges and bread.

PER SERVING *177 cal., 15 g fat (5 g sat. fat), 81 mg chol., 185 mg sodium, 3 g carb., 0 g fiber, 9 g pro.*

START TO FINISH **35 minutes**

8 servings	ingredients	16 servings
1 lb.	fresh or frozen large shrimp in shells	2 lb.
¼ cup	olive oil	½ cup
¼ cup	butter	½ cup
12	cloves garlic, smashed and peeled	24
4 sprigs	fresh thyme	8 sprigs
2	bay leaves	4
3 Tbsp.	dry sherry	6 Tbsp.
1 Tbsp.	paprika	2 Tbsp.
1 tsp.	Worcestershire sauce	2 tsp.
½ tsp.	kosher salt	1 tsp.
	Lemon wedges	
	Crusty French bread slices	

Quick Roasted Salt and Pepper Shrimp

It doesn't get any simpler than this—fresh shrimp is seasoned with olive oil, black pepper, and salt and blasted in a hot oven for just a few minutes. For the best flavor, be sure to use freshly ground black pepper.

1. Preheat oven to 400°F. Thaw shrimp, if frozen. Peel and devein shrimp, leaving tails intact if desired. Rinse shrimp; pat dry with paper towels.

2. Place shrimp in a 15×10×1-inch baking pan. Drizzle with oil; sprinkle with pepper and salt. Toss to coat. Roast, uncovered, for 8 to 10 minutes or until shrimp are opaque.

PER SERVING *96 cal., 3 g fat (0 g sat. fat), 143 mg chol., 765 mg sodium, 1 g carb., 0 g fiber, 15 g pro.*

PREP **20 minutes**
ROAST **8 minutes at 400°F**

8 servings	ingredients	16 servings
2 lb.	fresh or frozen jumbo shrimp in shells	4 lb.
1 Tbsp.	olive oil	2 Tbsp.
¾ tsp.	freshly ground black pepper	1½ tsp.
½ tsp.	kosher salt	1 tsp.

Goat Cheese-Olive Bites

To clean leeks—which can harbor grit and sand—cut the white part in half horizontally, then run cool water into the leek halves, fanning them to get all of the layers. Shake dry and slice thin.

1. Allow piecrust to stand according to package directions. Preheat oven to 375°F. Line a large baking sheet with parchment paper. Place piecrust on prepared baking sheet; roll into an 11-inch circle. Set aside.

2. For filling, in a medium skillet cook leek and fennel in hot oil over medium heat for 5 to 6 minutes or until tender, stirring occasionally. Remove from heat. Stir in cheese, olives, and thyme. Cool slightly.

3. Spread filling in center of pastry, leaving 1½ inches of pastry edges uncovered. Fold pastry edges up over filling.

4. Bake for 30 to 35 minutes or until pastry is golden brown. Cut into wedges and serve warm.

MAKE-AHEAD DIRECTIONS Prepare as directed through Step 3. Cover and chill up to 24 hours. Continue as directed in Step 4.

PER SERVING *272 cal., 18 g fat (7 g sat. fat), 18 mg chol., 347 mg sodium, 21 g carb., 1 g fiber, 5 g pro.*

PREP **25 minutes**
BAKE **30 minutes at 375°F**

6 servings	ingredients	12 servings
½ (1 crust)	15-oz. pkg. rolled refrigerated unbaked piecrust	1 (2 crusts)
1 cup	finely chopped leek (white part only)	2 cups
½ cup	finely chopped fennel	1 cup
1 Tbsp.	olive oil	2 Tbsp.
¾ cup (3 oz.)	crumbled aged goat cheese (chèvre) (such as Tumalo Farms Fenacho) or shredded Parmesan cheese	1½ cups (6 oz.)
¾ cup	coarsely chopped Gaeta, Kalamata, or other Italian olives	1½ cups
1 Tbsp.	snipped fresh thyme	2 Tbsp.

Petite Pesto-Parmesan Potatoes

Pancetta is unsmoked Italian-style bacon that usually comes in round slices. If you can't find it, you can substitute regular American-style bacon.

1. Preheat oven to 425°F. Scrub potatoes with a vegetable brush; pat dry with paper towels. Prick potatoes with a fork. For 20 servings, arrange potatoes in a 15×10×1-inch baking pan. Bake for 20 to 30 minutes or until tender, stirring once.

2. Meanwhile, in a small skillet cook pancetta over medium heat until crisp. Drain pancetta on paper towels, discarding drippings.

3. When potatoes are cool enough to handle, cut potatoes in half lengthwise. If necessary, cut a thin slice from each bottom to keep potato upright. Using a very small spoon or measuring teaspoon, scoop potato pulp out of each half, leaving a ¼-inch-thick shell. Place in a medium bowl.

4. Mash potato pulp with potato masher or electric mixer on low. Add sour cream, chives, salt, and, pepper; whip until smooth. Spoon filling over pesto. Place filled potato halves in a 3-quart rectangular baking dish. Sprinkle with pancetta.

5. Bake about 5 minutes or until heated through. Sprinkle with cheese. Bake about 2 minutes more or until cheese is melted. If desired, garnish with additional chives and cracked pepper.

FOR 40 SERVINGS Prepare using method above, except in Step 1 use two baking pans and in Step 4 use two baking dishes.

PER SERVING *47 cal., 2 g fat (1 g sat. fat), 4 mg chol., 90 mg sodium, 5 g carb., 1 g fiber, 1 g pro.*

PREP 50 minutes
BAKE 27 minutes at 425°F

20 servings	ingredients	40 servings
10 (1¼ lb.)	tiny new potatoes	20 (2½ lb.)
2 oz.	pancetta, chopped	4 oz.
⅓ cup	light sour cream	⅔ cup
1 tsp.	snipped fresh chives	2 tsp.
⅛ tsp.	salt	¼ tsp.
⅛ tsp.	cracked black pepper	¼ tsp.
2 Tbsp.	refrigerated basil pesto	¼ cup
2 Tbsp.	shredded Parmesan cheese	¼ cup
	Snipped fresh chives (optional)	
	Cracked black pepper (optional)	

Hoisin-Garlic Mushrooms

Chinese hoisin sauce is a one-stop flavor shop—it's sweet, salty, and spicy, all at once.

1. For 10 servings, in a 3½- or 4-quart slow cooker combine hoisin sauce, the water, garlic, and crushed red pepper. Add whole mushrooms and sweet pepper chunks. Stir to coat.

2. Cover and cook on low-heat setting for 5 to 6 hours or on high-heat setting for 2½ to 3 hours.

3. Using a slotted spoon, remove mushrooms and pepper chunks from cooker; discard sauce. If desired, garnish with green onion slices.

FOR 20 SERVINGS Prepare using method above, except in Step 1 use a 5- to 6-quart slow cooker.

PER SERVING *51 cal., 1 g fat (0 g sat. fat), 0 mg chol., 211 mg sodium, 9 g carb., 1 g fiber, 3 g pro.*

PREP **15 minutes**
SLOW COOK **5 hours (low) or 2½ hours (high)**

10 servings	ingredients	20 servings
½ cup	hoisin sauce	1 cup
¼ cup	water	½ cup
2 Tbsp. (6 cloves)	bottled minced garlic	¼ cup (12 cloves)
¼ to ½ tsp.	crushed red pepper	½ to 1 tsp.
24 oz.	fresh whole mushrooms, cleaned and trimmed	48 oz.
1 large	red sweet pepper, stemmed, seeded, and cut into chunks	2 large
	Thinly sliced green onions (optional)	

Spicy Roast Almonds

These crunchy, savory nuts can be made a few days before you need them. Be sure they are completely cool before storing them in a tightly sealed container so they stay crisp.

1. Preheat oven to 350°F. Evenly spread almonds in an ungreased 15×10×1-inch baking pan. Bake about 10 minutes or until lightly toasted, stirring once.

2. Meanwhile, in a small saucepan heat butter and oil over medium-low heat. Stir in Worcestershire sauce, cumin, garlic powder, salt, and cayenne pepper. Drizzle over warm almonds; toss gently to coat. Bake for 7 minutes. Spread nuts on a large sheet of foil; cool completely.

PER SERVING *229 cal., 20 g fat (2 g sat. fat), 3 mg chol., 116 mg sodium, 7 g carb., 4 g fiber, 8 g pro.*

PREP **10 minutes**
BAKE **17 minutes at 350°F**

6 servings	ingredients	12 servings
1½ cups	whole almonds	3 cups
1½ tsp.	butter	1 Tbsp.
1½ tsp.	olive oil	1 Tbsp.
1 Tbsp.	Worcestershire sauce	2 Tbsp.
½ tsp.	ground cumin	1 tsp.
½ tsp.	garlic powder	1 tsp.
¼ tsp.	kosher salt	½ tsp.
¼ tsp.	cayenne pepper	½ tsp.

Muffuletta Dip

The elements of the classic New Orleans sandwich—giardiniera, cheese, deli meats, and olives—give Big Easy flavor to this creamy slow cooker dip.

1. Rinse and drain pickled vegetables. Remove stems from peppers; chop vegetables (for 22 servings, you should have about 1 cup). In a 1½- or 2-quart slow cooker, combine pickled vegetables, cream cheese, provolone cheese, ham, olives, garlic, Italian seasoning, and, if desired, crushed red pepper.

2. Cover and cook on low-heat setting for 2 to 3 hours. Stir until cream cheese is smooth. Stir in enough milk (2 to 3 tablespoons) to reach dipping consistency.

3. Serve immediately or keep warm, covered, on warm setting or low-heat setting up to 2 hours, stirring occasionally and adding milk as necessary. Serve with salami on toasted bread.

FOR 44 SERVINGS Prepare using method above, except in Step 1 use a 3½- or 4-quart slow cooker.

PER SERVING *140 cal., 12 g fat (6 g sat. fat), 34 mg chol., 840 mg sodium, 4 g carb., 0 g fiber, 6 g pro.*

PREP **25 minutes**
SLOW COOK **2 hours (low)**

22 servings	ingredients	44 servings
1	16-oz. jar pickled mixed vegetables (giardiniera)	2
1	8-oz. pkg. cream cheese, cut up	2
1 cup (4 oz.)	shredded provolone cheese	2 cup (8 oz.)
2 oz.	cooked ham, finely chopped	4 oz.
½ cup	pitted Kalamata and/or green olives, rinsed, drained, and chopped	1 cup
2 cloves	garlic, minced	4 cloves
1 tsp.	dried Italian seasoning, crushed	2 tsp.
¼ tsp.	crushed red pepper (optional)	½ tsp.
	Milk	
	Thinly sliced salami	
	Small ciabatta rolls, halved and toasted, or focaccia squares	

Ham and Cheese Dip

Choose your favorite kind of ham—smoked, brown sugar, or honey—to use in this delightfully decadent dip. A swirl of honey mustard gives it a slightly sweet and piquant flavor.

1. For 22 servings, in a 1½- or 2-quart slow cooker combine ham, cream cheese, Swiss cheese, onions, wine, and honey mustard.

2. Cover and cook on high-heat setting for 1 to 2 hours or until cheeses are melted, stirring after 1 hour. Serve immediately or keep warm, covered, on warm setting or low-heat setting up to 2 hours, stirring occasionally. Serve with toast points.

FOR 44 SERVINGS Prepare using method above, except in Step 1 use a 3½- or 4-quart slow cooker.

PER SERVING 150 cal., 11 g fat (6 g sat. fat), 39 mg chol., 258 mg sodium, 5 g carb., 1 g fiber, 6 g pro.

PREP 20 minutes
SLOW COOK 1 hour (high)

22 servings	ingredients	44 servings
1 lb.	cooked ham, finely chopped	2 lb.
2	8-oz. pkg. cream cheese, cut up	4
2 cups (8 oz.)	shredded Swiss or Gruyère cheese	4 cups (16 oz.)
2 cups (2 large)	chopped sweet onions (such as Vidalia or Walla Walla)	4 cups (4 large)
½ cup	dry white wine or chicken broth	1 cup
2 Tbsp.	honey mustard	¼ cup
	Toast points	

Spinach Dip

Spinach dip is wildly popular for nearly any kind of party. There are multiple hot versions that are served with pita or tortilla chips. For a change of pace, try this flavorful chilled version served with crunchy vegetables.

1. In a medium mixing bowl combine cream cheese, sour cream, spinach, cheese, chives, lemon peel, lemon juice, garlic powder, salt, and cayenne pepper. Beat with an electric mixer on low speed until fluffy. Stir in radishes.

2. Cover and chill for 1 to 24 hours. Serve dip with sliced vegetables.

PER SERVING *69 cal., 6 g fat (4 g sat. fat), 19 mg chol., 110 mg sodium, 2 g carb., 0 g fiber, 2 g pro.*

PREP 25 minutes
CHILL 1 hour

20 servings	ingredients	40 servings
1	8-oz. pkg. cream cheese, softened	2
1	8-oz. carton sour cream	2
½	10-oz. pkg. frozen chopped spinach, thawed and well drained	1
¼ cup (1 oz.)	finely shredded Parmesan cheese	½ cup 2 oz.)
2 Tbsp.	snipped fresh chives	¼ cup
½ tsp.	finely shredded lemon peel	1 tsp.
1 Tbsp.	lemon juice	2 Tbsp.
½ tsp.	garlic powder	1 tsp.
¼ tsp.	salt	½ tsp.
¼ tsp.	cayenne pepper	½ tsp.
4 to 6	radishes, cut into thin bite-size strips	8 to 12
	Sliced carrots, radishes, and/or celery	

Edamame-Avocado Dip

This twist on traditional guacamole features edamame—a nutritional powerhouse. The flavor is brightened with pesto and fresh lemon juice.

START TO FINISH 20 minutes

10 servings	ingredients	20 servings
½	12-oz. pkg. frozen shelled sweet soybeans (edamame), thawed	1
½	medium avocado, seeded, peeled, and cut up	1
2 Tbsp.	chopped onion	¼ cup
4 tsp.	lemon juice	3 Tbsp.
1 Tbsp.	basil pesto	2 Tbsp.
⅛ tsp.	sea salt or kosher salt	¼ tsp.
⅛ tsp.	freshly ground black pepper	¼ tsp.
	Chopped tomato (optional)	
	Sea salt or kosher salt	
	Freshly ground black pepper	
	Pita chips or tortilla chips	

1. In a food processor combine edamame, avocado, onion, lemon juice, pesto, salt, and pepper. Cover and process until nearly smooth. Transfer to an airtight container; cover. Chill until ready to serve.

2. To serve, sprinkle dip with tomato (if desired) and additional salt and pepper. Serve with pita chips.

PER SERVING *48 cal., 3 g fat (0 g sat. fat), 0 g chol., 74 mg sodium, 3 g carb., 1 g fiber, 2 g pro.*

Cheese and Almond Guacamole

Here's a tip for getting the best, blemish-free avocados: Buy them when they are bright green and not yet ripe—and more resistant to bruising. Let them sit on the counter for a few days until they darken and yield slightly to gentle pressure.

1. In a large bowl combine avocados, onion, and serrano peppers; mash slightly with a fork. Fold in the cheese, almonds, cilantro, lime juice, and salt. Spoon into a serving bowl. Serve at once or cover surface with plastic wrap and chill up to 6 hours.

2. Serve with carrots, jicama, flatbread, and/or lime wedges. If desired, garnish guacamole with a cilantro sprig.

*TIP To toast whole nuts or large pieces, spread them in a shallow pan. Bake at 350°F for 5 to 10 minutes, shaking the pan once or twice. Toast coconut in the same way, watching closely to avoid burning. Toast finely chopped or ground nuts or sesame seeds in a dry skillet over medium heat. Stir often to prevent burning.

PER SERVING *183 cal., 16 g fat (5 g sat. fat), 13 mg chol., 268 mg sodium, 8 g carb., 5 g fiber, 6 g pro.*

START TO FINISH **20 minutes**

10 servings	ingredients	20 servings
4	medium avocados, halved, seeded, peeled, and coarsely chopped	8
½ cup	chopped red onion	1 cup
2	fresh serrano peppers, halved, seeded (if desired), and finely chopped (see tip, page 10)	4
¾ cup	crumbled feta cheese or goat cheese	1½ cups
½ cup	sliced almonds, toasted* and coarsely chopped	1 cup
⅓ cup	chopped fresh cilantro	⅔ cup
2 Tbsp.	lime juice	¼ cup
¾ tsp.	salt	1½ tsp.
	Carrots, jicama strips, flatbread, and/or lime wedges	
	Cilantro sprig (optional)	

Baked Asiago Hummus

This adaptation of a favorite appetizer incorporates caramelized onions and cheese into the classic creamy Middle-Eastern bean dip—and then serves it up warm.

1. Preheat oven to 450°F. For caramelized onion, in a large skillet melt butter over medium heat. Add onion and sugar; reduce heat to medium-low. Cook and stir for 20 to 25 minutes or until onion slices are very tender and caramelized. Coarsely chop; set aside.

2. For hummus, in a food processor combine beans, water, olive oil, sesame oil, garlic, snipped rosemary, salt, and pepper. Cover and process until smooth. Stir in two-thirds of the cheese. For 6 servings, transfer to a 12- to 16-ounce casserole dish.

3. Top hummus with caramelized onion and remaining cheese. Bake for 8 to 10 minutes or until cheese is browned and hummus is heated through. Garnish with rosemary sprig. Serve with baguette slices and carrot and celery sticks.

*TIP If desired, brush baguette slices with extra virgin olive oil before toasting.

FOR 12 SERVINGS Prepare using method above, except in Step 2 use two 12- to 16-ounce casserole dishes.

PER SERVING *183 cal., 10 g fat (4 g sat. fat), 13 mg chol., 427 mg sodium, 18 g carb., 3 g fiber, 6 g pro.*

PREP 15 minutes
COOK 20 minutes
BAKE 8 minutes at 450°F

6 servings	ingredients	12 servings
1 Tbsp.	butter	2 Tbsp.
1	onion, thinly sliced	2
½ tsp.	sugar	1 tsp.
1	15-oz. can garbanzo beans, rinsed and drained	2
2 Tbsp.	water	¼ cup
1 Tbsp.	olive oil	2 Tbsp.
1 Tbsp.	sesame oil	2 Tbsp.
1	garlic clove	2
½ tsp.	snipped fresh rosemary	1 tsp.
½ tsp.	salt	1 tsp.
¼ tsp.	black pepper	½ tsp.
6 Tbsp.	shredded Asiago cheese	¾ cup
	Fresh rosemary sprig (optional)	
	Toasted baguette slices, carrot sticks, and/or celery sticks	

CHAPTER 2

Poultry

Chicken and turkey are versatile birds—they lend themselves to a variety of preparations and cooking methods, from homey to refined.

37

45

58

Chicken-Green Olive Enchilada Casserole

This dish has the creamy texture and rich, spicy flavor of chicken enchiladas—without all of the stuffing and rolling. The ingredients are simply layered and baked until bubbly.

1. For sauce, in a large saucepan cook onion, garlic, oregano, cumin, and cinnamon in hot oil over medium heat about 4 minutes or until onion is tender. Stir in flour and chili powder; cook and stir for 3 minutes. Add broth in a slow steady stream, whisking to blend. Bring to boiling; reduce heat. For 6 servings, simmer, uncovered, about 15 minutes or until sauce is reduced to 1½ cups, stirring occasionally. Remove from heat; whisk in chocolate until melted.

2. Preheat oven to 375°F. Spread ⅓ cup of sauce in a greased 1½-quart rectangular baking dish. Arrange tortillas over sauce, overlapping as needed. Arrange half the shredded chicken over sauce; sprinkle with half the olives. Drizzle half the remaining sauce; spread as evenly as possible. Top sauce with half the cheese. Repeat layers, ending with cheese.

3. Cover tightly with greased foil. Bake about 40 minutes or until hot and bubbly.

FOR 12 SERVINGS Prepare using method above, except in Step 1 reduce the sauce to 3 cups. In Step 2 spread about ¾ cup sauce in a greased 3-quart baking dish. Arrange tortillas over the sauce and layer as above.

PER SERVING *309 cal., 16 g fat (7 g sat. fat), 70 mg chol., 594 mg sodium, 19 g carb., 3 g fiber, 24 g pro.*

PREP **30 minutes**
BAKE **40 minutes at 375°F**

6 servings	ingredients	12 servings
½ cup	finely chopped onion	1 cup
3 cloves	garlic, minced	6 cloves
1 tsp.	dried oregano, crushed	2 tsp.
1 tsp.	ground cumin	2 tsp.
⅛ tsp.	ground cinnamon	¼ tsp.
4 tsp.	vegetable oil	3 Tbsp.
4 tsp.	all-purpose flour	3 Tbsp.
1 Tbsp.	chili powder	2 Tbsp.
1	14.5-oz. can chicken broth	2
½ oz.	semisweet chocolate, finely chopped	1 oz.
6	6-inch corn tortillas	12
2 cups	shredded cooked chicken breasts	4 cups
¼ cup	pimiento-stuffed green olives, coarsely chopped	½ cup
1½ cups	shredded asadero or Monterey Jack cheese	3 cups
	Halved red and/or yellow cherry tomatoes	

Three-Cheese Ziti and Smoked Chicken Casserole

Look for smoked chicken in the deli department of your supermarket, close to the same spot the rotisserie chickens turn on their spits. If you can't find smoked chicken, regular roasted chicken works just fine.

PREP 25 minutes
BAKE 25 minutes at 375°F
STAND 10 minutes

6 servings	ingredients	12 servings
12 oz.	dried cut ziti pasta	24 oz.
3 Tbsp.	butter	6 Tbsp.
2	garlic cloves, minced	4
3 Tbsp.	all-purpose flour	6 Tbsp.
¼ tsp.	salt	½ tsp.
¼ tsp.	ground white pepper	½ tsp.
3½ cups	milk	7 cups
1½ cups (6 oz.)	finely shredded Asiago cheese	3 cups (12 oz.)
1 cup (4 oz.)	finely shredded Fontina cheese	2 cups (8 oz.)
½ cup (2 oz.)	crumbled blue cheese	1 cup (4 oz.)
2 cups	chopped smoked chicken or shredded purchased roasted chicken	4 cups
⅓ cup	panko bread crumbs or fine dry bread crumbs	⅔ cup
2 tsp.	truffle-flavor oil or melted butter	4 tsp.

1. Preheat oven to 375°F. For 6 servings, grease a 2-quart casserole; set aside. Cook pasta according to package directions; drain. Return pasta to pan.

2. Meanwhile, in a medium saucepan melt butter over medium heat. Add garlic; cook and stir for 30 seconds. Stir in flour, salt, and white pepper. Gradually stir in milk. Cook and stir until thickened and bubbly. Gradually add Asiago cheese, fontina cheese, and blue cheese, stirring until melted. Stir in chicken. Add chicken mixture to cooked pasta; stir gently to combine.

3. Transfer pasta mixture to prepared casserole. In a small bowl combine panko and truffle oil; sprinkle over pasta mixture. Bake, uncovered, about 25 minutes or until heated through and crumbs are light brown. Let stand for 10 minutes before serving.

FOR 12 SERVINGS Prepare using method above, except in Step 1 grease a 4-quart casserole.

PER SERVING *753 cal., 39 g fat (22 g sat. fat), 141 mg chol., 953 mg sodium, 56 g carb., 2 g fiber, 43 g pro.*

Balsamic-Glazed Chicken Tenders

The surprising base for the sauce is cinnamon applesauce. Infused with a shot of balsamic vinegar and cardamom, it makes a glossy glaze and nicely spiced crust on the chicken.

1. Finely shred peel from orange; set aside. Juice orange. For balsamic sauce, in a medium saucepan combine applesauce, vinegar, cardamom, juice from the orange, salt, and pepper. Bring to boiling over high heat. Reduce heat to low. Cook, uncovered, stirring occasionally for 10 minutes. Remove from heat; cover to keep warm.

2. Lightly season chicken with salt and pepper. Heat oil in an extra-large nonstick skillet over medium-high heat. Add chicken; cook until golden brown on bottom, about 4 minutes. Turn chicken and add ½ cup of the balsamic sauce to skillet. Cook 2 to 3 minutes or until chicken is cooked through.

3. To serve, top chicken with some balsamic sauce, orange peel, and, if desired, fresh thyme. Pass remaining sauce.

*TIP If desired, for 4 servings, use ¼ teaspoon ground nutmeg instead of ½ teaspoon cardamom. For 8 servings, use ½ teaspoon ground nutmeg instead of 1 teaspoon ground cardamom.

PER SERVING *208 cal., 4 g fat (1 g sat. fat), 66 mg chol., 207 mg sodium, 15 g carb., 1 g fiber, 27 g pro.*

START TO FINISH **25 minutes**

4 servings	ingredients	8 servings
1	small orange	2
⅔ cup	cinnamon applesauce	1⅓ cups
¼ cup	balsamic vinegar	½ cup
½ tsp.	ground cardamom*	1 tsp.
½ tsp.	salt	1 tsp.
½ tsp.	black pepper	1 tsp.
1 lb.	chicken tenders	2 lb.
	Salt	
	Black pepper	
2 tsp.	vegetable oil	4 tsp.
	Fresh thyme sprigs (optional)	

Saucy BBQ Chicken

Serve lots of napkins with this sweet and delightfully sloppy oven-broiled chicken.

1. Preheat broiler. Broil chicken on the unheated rack of a broiler pan 4 to 5 inches from heat for 10 minutes.

2. Lightly brush onion slices with olive oil. Remove broiler pan from oven. Turn and move chicken to one end of pan. Place onion slices in a single layer on opposite end of pan. Broil for 15 minutes or until chicken is no longer pink and juices run clear (180°F).

3. Meanwhile, for barbecue sauce, in a medium saucepan combine ketchup, molasses, vinegar, brown sugar, paprika, and pepper sauce. Bring to boiling over medium heat. Remove from heat; keep warm. Remove onions from broiler. Broil chicken 2 minutes more; brush with some of the sauce during the last minute.

4. Chop two of the onion slices; stir into remaining sauce. Serve chicken with sauce, onion slices, and parsley.

PER SERVING *426 cal., 16 g fat (4 g sat. fat), 118 mg chol., 802 mg sodium, 41 g carb., 1 g fiber, 30 g pro.*

START TO FINISH **30 minutes**

4 servings	ingredients	8 servings
8	small chicken drumsticks	16
1	large onion, cut into 6 slices	2
	Olive oil	
1 cup	ketchup	2 cups
¼ cup	molasses	½ cup
¼ cup	cider vinegar	½ cup
2 Tbsp.	packed brown sugar	¼ cup
1 tsp.	smoked paprika	2 tsp.
	Several dashes bottled hot pepper sauce	
	Fresh parsley	

Chicken and Vegetable Sauté

This vibrantly hued, one-pot meal is packed with veggies and lean protein. A generous serving contains just 356 calories and 6 grams of fat.

START TO FINISH 30 minutes

4 servings	ingredients	8 servings
2 cups	broccoli florets	4 cups
4	medium carrots, cut lengthwise into strips	8
1 Tbsp.	olive oil	2 Tbsp.
4 (1¼ lb.)	skinless, boneless chicken breast halves, cut lengthwise into thirds	8 (2½ lb.)
	Salt	
	Black pepper	
½	medium red onion, cut into thin wedges	1
1	15-oz. can Great Northern beans, rinsed and drained	2
½ cup	reduced-sodium chicken broth	1 cup
1 Tbsp.	finely shredded lemon peel	2 Tbsp.

1. For 4 servings, in a 3-quart saucepan cook broccoli and carrots in boiling salted water about 3 minutes or until crisp-tender. Drain vegetables and place in a bowl of ice water to halt cooking. When cool, drain; set aside.

2. In an extra-large nonstick skillet heat oil over medium-high heat. Sprinkle chicken with salt and pepper. Cook chicken in hot oil for 10 to 12 minutes or until no longer pink (170°F), turning occasionally. Remove from skillet.

3. Reduce heat to medium-low. Add onion to hot skillet; sprinkle with additional salt and pepper. Cook and stir for 2 minutes. Increase heat to medium-high. Add beans, broth, lemon peel, vegetables, and chicken. Cook and stir about 1 minute or until heated through.

FOR 8 SERVINGS Prepare using method above, except in Step 1 use a 6-quart Dutch oven.

PER SERVING *356 cal., 6 g fat (1 g sat. fat), 82 mg chol., 587 mg sodium, 33 g carb., 8 g fiber, 43 g pro.*

Mediterranean Chicken and Polenta

There's actually no need to buy a product labeled "polenta" (though it's fine if you do). Polenta is simply cornmeal that is cooked in water, milk, or broth until it smooth and creamy. Stir in a little butter and Parmesan cheese after it has cooked if you like.

1. Preheat oven to 375°F. Drain tomatoes, reserving the oil. Sprinkle chicken with salt and pepper. In a large oven-going skillet heat the reserved oil over medium-high heat. Add chicken; cook about 6 minutes or until browned, turning once. Remove skillet from heat. Add tomatoes, olives, wine, and, if desired, bay leaves.

2. Bake for 10 to 15 minutes or until an instant-read thermometer inserted in center of chicken breast halves registers 170°F.

3. Meanwhile, for polenta, in a large saucepan bring 3 cups water to boiling. In a small bowl combine cornmeal, 1 cup cold water, and 1 teaspoon salt; gradually stir into boiling water. Cook and stir until thick and bubbly. Reduce heat; cook for 10 minutes more, stirring occasionally.

4. To serve, spoon polenta into shallow bowls. If using, remove and discard bay leaves from chicken, Top polenta with chicken and tomato mixture. Sprinkle with thyme if desired.

PER SERVING *370 cal., 8 g fat (1 g sat. fat), 66 mg chol., 575 mg sodium, 46 g carb., 3 g fiber, 30 g pro.*

PREP **15 minutes**
BAKE **10 minutes at 375°F**

4 servings	ingredients	8 servings
½	6.5-oz. jar oil-pack dried tomatoes with Italian herbs	1
4 (1 to 1¼ lb.)	small skinless, boneless chicken breast halves	8 (2 to 2½ lb.)
	Salt and black pepper	
1 cup	assorted olives, drained	2 cups
½ cup	dry white wine or reduced-sodium chicken broth	1 cup
4	small bay leaves (optional)	8
1 cup	cornmeal	2 cups
1 cup	water	2 cups
1 tsp.	salt	2 tsp.
	Fresh thyme sprigs (optional)	

Tuscany Stuffed Chicken Breasts

Sage, sweet peppers, and white wine give these beautiful cheese-stuffed chicken breasts the Tuscan touch.

4 servings	ingredients	8 servings
	START TO FINISH 30 minutes	
4	skinless, boneless chicken breast halves (about 4 oz. each)	8
	Black pepper	
4 oz.	Fontina cheese, crumbled or sliced	8 oz.
1 cup	bottled roasted red sweet peppers, drained	2 cups
12	fresh sage leaves*	24
¼ cup	all-purpose flour	½ cup
2 Tbsp.	olive oil	¼ cup
1 cup	dry white wine or chicken broth	2 cups

1. Place each chicken piece, boned side up, between two pieces of plastic wrap. Using the flat side of a meat mallet and working from the center to the edges, lightly pound chicken to about ¼-inch thickness. Remove plastic wrap. Sprinkle chicken with black pepper. Layer cheese, roasted red sweet peppers, and sage in the center of each breast. Fold in edges; roll into a spiral, pressing edges to seal. Place flour in a shallow dish; dip chicken roll-ups in flour, turning to coat.

2. Heat oil in a large skillet over medium heat. Cook chicken for 5 minutes or until brown, turning to brown evenly. Remove chicken from skillet.

3. In the same skillet bring wine or broth to boiling; reduce heat. For 4 servings, simmer, uncovered, about 2 minutes or until liquid is reduced to ½ cup. Return chicken to skillet. Cover and simmer for 7 to 8 minutes or until chicken is tender and no longer pink. To serve, spoon cooking liquid over chicken.

*TIP If desired, for 4 servings, use 1 teaspoon dried sage, crushed, for the 12 fresh sage leaves. For 8 servings, use 2 teaspoons dried sage, crushed, for the 24 sage leaves.

FOR 8 SERVINGS Prepare using method above, except in Step 3 reduce liquid to 1 cup.

PER SERVING *364 cal., 19 g fat (7 g sat. fat), 92 mg chol., 284 mg sodium, 8 g carb., 1 g fiber, 30 g pro.*

Chicken and Potatoes with Lemon

Roasted lemons are used to make the vinaigrette for this dish of chicken, potatoes, and olives served warm on a bed of cool, crisp, and pleasantly peppery greens.

1. Preheat oven to 450°F. For 4 servings, place chicken, potatoes, lemons, and olives in an ungreased 3-quart rectangular baking dish. Drizzle with one-third of the oil; toss to coat. Spread in a single layer, arranging chicken skin sides up and lemons cut sides up. Sprinkle with salt and pepper.

2. Bake, uncovered, about 30 minutes or until chicken is no longer pink (170°F), potatoes are tender, and lemons are browned at the edges and soft throughout.

3. When lemons are cool enough to handle, squeeze juice and pulp into a small bowl. Discard any seeds. Whisk in the remaining oil and honey. Season to taste with salt and pepper. Cover chicken, potatoes, and olives to keep warm.

4. Divide arugula and/or mixed greens among dinner plates. Top with chicken, potatoes, and olives. Drizzle with lemon mixture. Sprinkle with additional pepper.

FOR 8 SERVINGS Prepare using method above, except in Step 1 use two 3-quart rectangular baking dishes, rotating pans halfway through baking time.

PER SERVING *573 cal., 40 g fat (8 g sat. fat), 87 mg chol., 435 mg sodium, 34 g carb., 7 g fiber, 26 g pro.*

PREP **20 minutes**
BAKE **30 minutes at 450°F**

4 servings	ingredients	8 servings
4 (1½ lb. total)	bone-in chicken breast halves	8 (3 lb. total)
1 lb.	fingerling or baby Yukon gold potatoes	2 lb.
3	lemons, halved crosswise	6
⅓ cup	pitted green and/or black olives	⅔ cup
6 Tbsp.	olive oil	¾ cup
	Salt	
	Black pepper	
1 Tbsp.	honey	2 Tbsp.
6 cups	arugula and/or mixed salad greens	12 cups

Seared Chicken with Cherry-Tarragon Sauce

Tarragon is often paired with fruit in sauces for poultry. It has a fairly intense licorice flavor; if you like your licoricey herbs on the milder side, use fresh basil instead.

1. For 4 servings, in a shallow dish stir together flour, paprika, dry mustard, the ¼ teaspoon salt, and the ¼ teaspoon pepper. Dip chicken into flour mixture, turning to coat. In a large skillet cook chicken in hot oil over medium to medium-high heat for 8 to 10 minutes or until chicken is no longer pink (180°F), turning once. Remove from skillet; keep warm.

2. For sauce, add cherries, tarragon, and garlic to the same skillet. Cook and stir over medium heat for 1 minute. Stir in wine and broth. Simmer, uncovered, for 3 to 5 minutes or until sauce is reduced to about 2 cups. Stir in butter until melted. Season to taste with additional salt and pepper.

3. To serve, spoon sauce over chicken. Serve with couscous. If desired, sprinkle with additional tarragon.

FOR 8 SERVINGS Prepare using method above, except in Step 1 use ½ teaspoon each salt and pepper. In Step 2 reduce the sauce to 4 cups.

PER SERVING *573 cal., 21 g fat (7 g sat. fat), 180 mg chol., 631 mg sodium, 40 g carb., 3 g fiber, 44 g pro.*

START TO FINISH **30 minutes**

4 servings	ingredients	8 servings
¼ cup	all-purpose flour	½ cup
2 tsp.	smoked paprika	4 tsp.
1 tsp.	dry mustard	2 tsp.
¼ tsp.	salt	½ tsp.
¼ tsp.	ground black pepper	½ tsp.
8	skinless, boneless chicken thighs	16
2 Tbsp.	olive oil	¼ cup
2 cups	fresh or thawed, frozen pitted dark sweet cherries	4 cups
2 Tbsp.	snipped fresh tarragon or basil	¼ cup
3	cloves garlic, minced	6
1 cup	dry red wine or cherry juice	2 cups
½ cup	chicken broth	1 cup
2 Tbsp.	butter	4 Tbsp.
	Salt and black pepper	
2 cups	hot cooked couscous, rice, or pasta	4 cups
	Snipped fresh tarragon or basil (optional)	

Sesame-Ginger Barbecued Chicken

Be sure to brush the sauce on the chicken only during the last 5 minutes of grilling. If you try brushing it on any earlier, it will likely burn.

1. For sauce, in a small saucepan combine plum sauce, the water, hoisin sauce, sesame seeds, ginger, garlic, and chili sauce. Bring to boiling over medium heat, stirring frequently; reduce heat. Simmer, covered, for 3 minutes.

2. For a charcoal or gas grill, place chicken on the rack of a covered grill directly over medium heat. Grill for 12 to 15 minutes or until chicken is no longer pink (170°F for breasts; 180°F for thighs), turning once halfway through grilling and brushing with some of the sauce during the last 5 minutes of grilling.

3. Reheat the remaining sauce until boiling. If desired, serve with hot cooked noodles and sautéed green onion and carrot matchsticks.

*TIP If desired, for 6 servings, you may use ¼ teaspoon ground ginger in place of the 1 teaspoon grated fresh ginger. For 12 servings, you may use ½ teaspoon ground ginger in place of the 2 teaspoons grated fresh ginger.

PER SERVING *166 cal., 4 g fat (1 g sat. fat), 59 mg chol., 216 mg sodium, 9 g carb., 22 g pro.*

PREP 20 minutes
GRILL 12 minutes

6 servings	ingredients	12 servings
⅓ cup	plum sauce or sweet-and-sour sauce	⅔ cup
¼ cup	water	½ cup
3 Tbsp.	hoisin sauce	6 Tbsp.
1½ tsp.	sesame seeds, toasted if desired (see tip, page 28)	3 tsp.
1 tsp.	grated fresh ginger*	2 tsp.
1	clove garlic, minced	2
¼ to ½ tsp.	Asian chili sauce (Sriracha sauce) or several dashes bottled hot pepper sauce	½ to 1 tsp.
6	skinless, boneless chicken breast halves	12
	Hot cooked noodles (optional)	
	Green onion and carrot matchsticks, lightly sautéed (optional)	

Tequila-Marinated Chicken Thighs

The marinade of tequila, orange juice, lime juice, oregano, garlic, and smoky chipotle chiles gives deep flavor to these grilled chicken thighs.

1. Place chicken in a resealable plastic bag set in a shallow dish. For marinade, in a small bowl combine orange juice, tequila, lime juice, chipotle pepper, oregano, garlic, salt, and black pepper. Pour marinade over chicken. Seal bag; turn to coat chicken. Marinate in the refrigerator for 4 to 6 hours, turning bag occasionally. Drain chicken, reserving marinade.

2. For a charcoal grill, arrange medium-hot coals around a drip pan. Test for medium heat above pan. Place chicken, meaty sides down, on grill rack over drip pan. Cover and grill for 50 to 60 minutes or until an instant-read thermometer reads 180°F, turning and brushing once with the reserved marinade halfway through grilling. (For a gas grill, preheat grill. Reduce heat to medium. Adjust for indirect cooking. Grill as above.) Discard any remaining marinade.

PER SERVING *432 cal., 29 g fat (8 g sat. fat), 158 mg chol., 349 mg sodium, 3 g carb., 0 g fiber, 33 g pro.*

PREP **15 minutes**
MARINATE **4 hours**
GRILL **50 minutes**

6 servings	ingredients	12 servings
12	bone-in chicken thighs, skinned if desired	24
½ cup	orange juice	1 cup
¼ cup	tequila	½ cup
2 Tbsp.	lime juice	¼ cup
1 Tbsp.	finely chopped canned chipotle pepper in adobo sauce	2 Tbsp.
1 tsp.	snipped fresh oregano	2 tsp.
2	cloves garlic, minced	4
½ tsp.	salt	1 tsp.
¼ tsp.	black pepper	½ tsp.

Crab-Stuffed Chicken

Just a little crabmeat goes a long way toward making a dish elegant. These chicken rolls stuffed with a filling of crabmeat, onion, mushrooms, and Swiss cheese are perfect for a dinner gathering.

PREP 45 minutes
BAKE 37 minutes at 350°F

4 servings	ingredients	8 servings
4	skinless, boneless chicken breasts	8
3 Tbsp.	butter	6 Tbsp.
2 Tbsp.	all-purpose flour	¼ cup
⅓ cup	milk	¾ cup
⅓ cup	chicken broth	¾ cup
2 Tbsp.	dry white wine	⅓ cup
½ cup	chopped fresh mushrooms	1 cup
2 Tbsp.	chopped onion	¼ cup
½	6-oz. can crabmeat, drained, flaked, and cartilage removed	1
¼ cup	coarsely crushed saltine crackers	½ cup
1 Tbsp.	snipped fresh parsley	2 Tbsp.
¼ tsp.	salt	½ tsp.
dash	black pepper	dash
½ cup (2 oz.)	shredded Swiss cheese	1 cup (4 oz.)
¼ tsp.	paprika	½ tsp.

1. Preheat oven to 350°F. Place each chicken breast half between two pieces of plastic wrap. Using the flat side of a meat mallet, lightly pound chicken to about ⅛-inch thickness. Remove plastic wrap.

2. For sauce, in a medium saucepan melt 4 teaspoons of the butter over medium heat. Stir in flour. Gradually stir in milk, broth, and wine. Cook and stir until thickened and bubbly.

3. For filling, in a medium skillet melt 2 teaspoons of the butter over medium heat. Add mushrooms and onion; cook until tender, stirring occasionally. Stir in crabmeat, crackers, parsley, salt, and pepper. Stir in 1 tablespoon of the sauce. Place about ¼ cup filling on each piece of chicken. Fold in sides; roll up chicken. If necessary, secure with wooden toothpicks. In a large skillet melt 1 tablespoon of the butter over medium heat. Cook chicken rolls, half at a time, in hot butter until brown on all sides.

4. Arrange chicken rolls, seam sides down, in a 1½-quart rectangular baking dish. Top with remaining sauce. Bake, covered, about 35 minutes or until chicken is no longer pink. Sprinkle with cheese and paprika. Bake, uncovered, 2 minutes more or until cheese is melted. Remove toothpicks, if using.

5. Transfer chicken to a serving platter. Whisk sauce in baking dish; pass with chicken.

FOR 8 SERVINGS Prepare using method above, except in Step 2 use 3 tablespoons butter. In Step 3 cook mushrooms and onion in 1 tablespoon butter and cook chicken rolls in 2 tablespoons melted butter. In Step 4 use a 3-quart rectangular baking dish.

PER SERVING *367 cal., 16 g fat (9 g sat. fat), 140 mg chol., 542 mg sodium, 9 g carb., 1 g fiber, 43 g pro.*

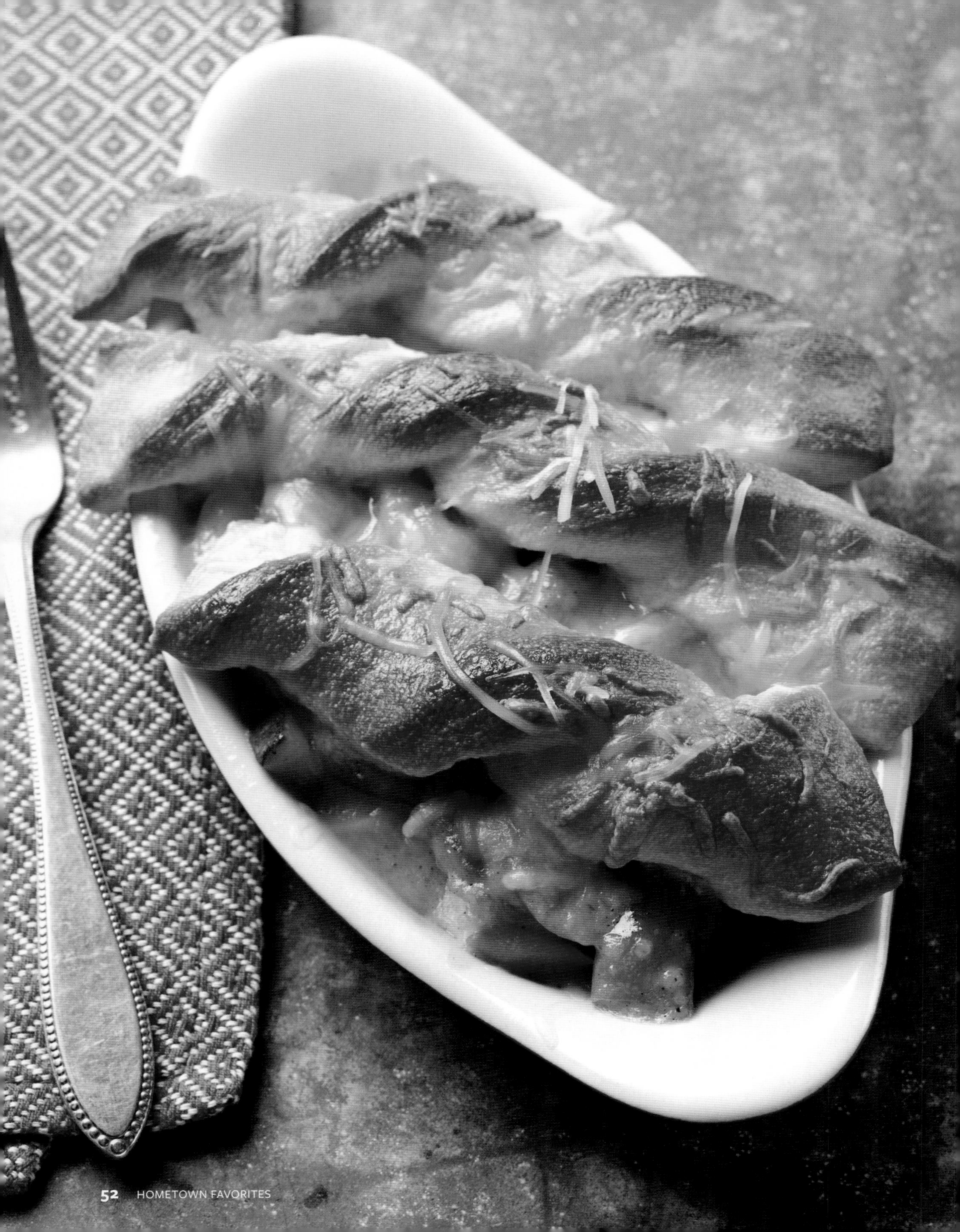

Chicken with Breadstick Twists

Cheese-topped refrigerated breadsticks make a super quick crust for these individual chicken-and-veggie casseroles.

1. Preheat oven to 400°F. In a large resealable plastic bag combine flour, sage, salt, and pepper. Cut chicken into bite-size pieces. Add chicken to bag; seal bag and shake to coat.

2. In a large skillet heat oil over medium-high heat. Add chicken to hot oil; sprinkle any remaining flour mixture over chicken. Cook chicken for 2 minutes (chicken will not be completely cooked), stirring to brown evenly. Place vegetables in a sieve or colander. Run cold water over vegetables to thaw. Add vegetables, broth, and milk to chicken in skillet. Bring to boiling, stirring once. Open package of breadsticks and separate into 12 pieces.

3. Divide chicken mixture among four 16-ounce gratin dishes or individual casseroles. Arrange three breadsticks across the top of each dish. Sprinkle with cheese. Bake for 18 minutes or until breadstick twists are browned and the filling is bubbly.

FOR 8 SERVINGS Prepare using method above, except in Step 3 use eight 16-ounce gratin or casserole dishes.

PER SERVING *544 cal., 17 g fat (7 g sat. fat), 64 mg chol., 1,138 mg sodium, 61 g carb., 4 g fiber, 35 g pro.*

PREP **20 minutes**
BAKE **18 minutes at 400°F**

4 servings	ingredients	8 servings
½ cup	all-purpose flour	1 cup
½ tsp.	ground sage	1 tsp.
¼ tsp.	salt	½ tsp.
¼ tsp.	black pepper	½ tsp.
12 oz.	skinless, boneless chicken breast halves	24 oz.
2 Tbsp.	vegetable oil	¼ cup
2 cups	frozen mixed vegetables	4 cups
1	14.5-oz. can reduced-sodium chicken broth	2
½ cup	milk	1 cup
1	11-oz. pkg. of 12 refrigerated breadsticks	2
½ cup (2 oz.)	shredded Mexican-style four-cheese blend	1 cup (4 oz.)

Easy Chicken Jambalaya

Use a mix of sweet peppers for the most eye-catching color in this flash-cooked version of a New Orleans favorite.

1. In a medium bowl combine chicken and Cajun seasoning; toss gently to coat.

2. Heat an extra-skillet over medium-high heat. Add chicken and sausage; cook for 3 to 4 minutes or until chicken begins to brown, stirring frequently. Add sweet peppers and onion; cook for 2 minutes more, stirring frequently.

3. Add stewed tomatoes, breaking up large pieces of tomato with a spoon. Cook, covered, for 5 to 7 minutes or until chicken is no longer pink. If desired, sprinkle each serving with parsley.

PER SERVING *355 cal., 18 g fat (5 g sat. fat), 81 mg chol., 637 mg sodium, 23 g carb., 3 g fiber, 29 g pro.*

START TO FINISH **25 minutes**

4 servings	ingredients	8 servings
8 oz.	skinless, boneless chicken breast halves, cut into 1-inch pieces	1 lb.
2 tsp.	Cajun seasoning	4 tsp.
8 oz.	cooked spicy or mild sausage, sliced	1 lb.
2	medium yellow, green, and/or orange sweet, peppers seeded and cut into bite-size strips	4
1	small red onion, cut into thin wedges	2
2	14.5-oz. cans no-salt-added stewed tomatoes, undrained	4
	Coarsely snipped fresh parsley (optional)	

Chicken Soup with Chive Dumplings

It doesn't get much more comforting than a bowl of homemade chicken soup topped with soft and buttery dumplings. Serve with a crisp green salad and dinner is done.

1. Sprinkle chicken with salt and pepper. In a large Dutch oven cook chicken in hot oil over medium-high heat until brown on both sides. Reduce heat to medium. Cook, covered, for 8 minutes or until an instant-read thermometer reads 170°F. Remove chicken; cool.

2. Add carrots, celery, and leeks to Dutch oven. Cook, covered, for 5 to 7 minutes or until vegetables are tender.

3. Cut chicken into ½-inch pieces. Return chicken to Dutch oven. Add stock, thyme, and bay leaf. Bring to boiling; reduce heat. Simmer, uncovered, for 15 minutes.

4. Meanwhile, for dumplings, in a medium bowl stir together flour, chives, baking powder, and salt. Using a pastry blender, cut in butter until mixture resembles coarse crumbs. Stir in milk just until combined.

5. Remove thyme and bay leaf from soup. Stir in parsley; season to taste with additional salt and pepper. Bring to boiling. Drop mounds of dough onto hot bubbling soup. Cook, uncovered, for 10 minutes. Reduce heat to medium-low. Cook, covered, about 10 minutes more or until a toothpick inserted in centers of dumplings comes out clean.

PER SERVING *334 cal., 12 g fat (5 g sat. fat), 62 mg chol., 1,260 mg sodium, 30 g carb., 2 g fiber, 24 g pro.*

PREP 30 minutes
COOK 50 minutes

6 servings	ingredients	12 servings
3 (about 1 lb.)	skinless, boneless chicken breast halves	6 (about 2 lb.)
	Salt	
	Black pepper	
2 Tbsp.	olive oil	¼ cup
1 cup	chopped carrots	2 cups
1 cup	chopped celery	2 cups
⅓ cup	chopped leeks	⅔ cup
6 cups	chicken stock	12 cups
4 sprigs	fresh thyme	8 sprigs
1	bay leaf	2
1½ cups	all-purpose flour	3 cups
1 Tbsp.	snipped fresh chives	2 Tbsp.
2 tsp.	baking powder	4 tsp.
1 tsp.	salt	2 tsp.
3 Tbsp.	cold butter	6 Tbsp.
¾ cup	milk	1½ cups
¼ cup	snipped fresh parsley	½ cup

Spring Chicken Stew

Baby bok choy is cleverly steamed as it sits on top of the chicken in this light spring stew. For the best taste and texture, cook the bok choy only until it is crisp-tender.

1. Finely shred peel from lemon; set peel aside. Juice lemon and set juice aside. Lightly sprinkle chicken with salt and pepper.

2. In a Dutch oven heat olive oil over medium-high heat; add chicken. Cook for 2 to 3 minutes or until chicken is browned, turning occasionally.

3. Add the water, gravy, carrots, and mustard to chicken in Dutch oven. Bring to boiling. Place bok choy on top. Reduce heat. Simmer, covered, about 10 minutes or until no pink remains in chicken and vegetables are tender. Add lemon juice to taste.

4. Ladle stew into bowls. Top with lemon peel and, if desired, lemon thyme.

PER SERVING *273 cal., 12 g fat (2 g sat. fat), 117 mg chol., 909 mg sodium, 13 g carb., 3 g fiber, 31 g pro.*

START TO FINISH **30 minutes**

4 servings	ingredients	8 servings
1	lemon	2
1¼ lb.	skinless, boneless chicken thighs	2½ lb.
	Salt	
	Black pepper	
1 Tbsp.	olive oil	2 Tbsp.
1½ cups	water	3 cups
1	12-oz. jar chicken gravy	2
8 oz.	baby carrots, halved lengthwise	1 lb.
1 Tbsp.	Dijon mustard	2 Tbsp.
2 heads	baby bok choy, quartered	4 heads
	Snipped fresh lemon thyme (optional)	

Corn and Chicken Chowder

PREP 30 minutes
COOK 20 minutes

4 servings	ingredients	8 servings
6	fresh ears of corn*	12
1 Tbsp.	vegetable oil	2 Tbsp.
¾ cup	chopped onion	1½ cups
¾ cup	chopped green and/or red sweet pepper	1½ cups
1	14.5-oz. can chicken broth	2
1 cup	cubed, peeled potato	2 cups
1 cup	half-and-half, light cream, or milk	2 cups
2 Tbsp.	all-purpose flour	¼ cup
2 tsp.	snipped fresh thyme	1 Tbsp.
¼ tsp.	salt	½ tsp.
¼ tsp.	black pepper	½ tsp.
1¼ cups	chopped cooked chicken	2½ cups
2 slices	bacon, crisp-cooked, drained, and crumbled	4 slices
	Fresh thyme sprigs (optional)	

The simplest way to cook the bacon is in the microwave: Layer it between two double layers of paper towels. Cook on high for about 2 minutes or until desired doneness. It will crisp as it cools.

1. If using fresh corn, use a sharp knife to cut corn kernels off the cobs; set aside. In a large saucepan heat oil over medium heat. Add onion and sweet pepper; cook until tender, stirring occasionally. Stir in broth, potato, and fresh or frozen corn. Bring to boiling; reduce heat. Simmer, covered, about 20 minutes or until potato is tender, stirring occasionally.

2. In a small bowl combine half-and-half, flour, snipped thyme, salt, and black pepper; stir into corn mixture. Cook and stir until thickened and bubbly. Cook and stir for 1 minute. Add chicken and bacon; cook and stir until heated through. If desired, garnish with thyme sprigs.

*TIP If desired, for 4 servings, use 3 cups frozen corn for the 6 fresh ears of corn. For 8 servings, use 6 cups frozen corn for the 12 fresh ears of corn.

PER SERVING *410 cal., 18 g fat (7 g sat. fat), 65 mg chol., 612 mg sodium, 43 g carb., 6 g fiber, 24 g pro.*

Crispy Chopped Chicken Salad

The crunch in this hearty main-dish salad comes from a variety of ingredients, including fresh zucchini, sweet pepper, carrot, Romaine lettuce—and crisp-cooked and crumbled prosciutto.

1. Preheat oven to 400°F. Place prosciutto in a single layer on a large baking sheet. Bake for 8 to 10 minutes or until crisp. Set aside.

2. Meanwhile, sprinkle chicken with salt, paprika, and black pepper. In a large nonstick skillet heat 1 tablespoon of the oil over medium heat. Add chicken; cook for 8 to 10 minutes or until an instant-read thermometer registers 170°F, turning once. Cool slightly; slice chicken.

3. For lemon dressing, finely shred peel from one of the lemons; squeeze juice from lemons to equal ⅓ cup. In a small bowl whisk together the remaining oil, lemon peel, lemon juice, and shallot. Season to taste with salt and black pepper.

4. In a large bowl combine chicken, zucchini, sweet peppers, carrot, and red onion. Add lemon dressing; toss gently to coat. Add cheese.

5. Line salad bowls with lettuce leaves. Top with chicken salad and sprinkle with prosciutto.

FOR 12 SERVINGS Prepare using method above, except in Step 2 use 2 tablespoons oil. In Step 3 squeeze lemons to equal ⅔ cup juice.

PER SERVING *425 cal., 28 g fat (8 g sat. fat), 86 mg chol., 965 mg sodium, 10 g carb., 2 g fiber, 34 g pro.*

PREP 45 minutes
BAKE 8 minutes at 400°F

6 servings	ingredients	12 servings
6 (about 4 oz.)	thin slices prosciutto	12 (about 8 oz.)
4	skinless, boneless chicken breast halves	8
	Salt	
	Paprika	
	Black pepper	
½ cup	olive oil	1 cup
2	lemons	4
2 Tbsp.	finely chopped shallot	¼ cup
2½ cups	chopped zucchini	5 cups
¾ cup	chopped red sweet pepper	1½ cups
¾ cup	chopped yellow sweet pepper	1½ cups
⅔ cup	thinly sliced carrot	1⅓ cups
3 Tbsp.	chopped red onion	6 Tbsp.
1¼ cups (5 oz.)	crumbled blue cheese	2½ cups (10 oz.)
	Romaine lettuce leaves	

Chicken, Tomato, and Cucumber Salad

This hearty salad is just the thing to serve on a hot summer night. Cool, crunchy ribbons of cucumber, ripe tomatoes, and quick-cooked chicken tenders are dressed with a simple herbed vinaigrette. Serve it with crusty bread for sopping up every last juicy bite.

START TO FINISH **25 minutes**

4 servings	ingredients	8 servings
5 Tbsp.	olive oil	10 Tbsp.
1 to 1¼ lb.	chicken breast tenders	2¼ to 2½ lb.
	Salt	
	Black pepper	
¼ cup	cider vinegar or white wine vinegar	½ cup
1 Tbsp.	snipped fresh thyme	2 Tbsp.
1 tsp.	sugar	2 tsp.
1	medium cucumber, cut into thin ribbons	2
2	tomatoes, sliced	4
½ cup	pitted green olives, halved and/or sliced	1 cup
4 oz.	feta cheese, crumbled (optional)	8 oz.

1. In a large skillet heat 1 tablespoon of the oil over medium heat. Lightly sprinkle chicken tenders with salt and pepper. Cook chicken in hot oil for 8 to 10 minutes or until no longer pink, turning once halfway through cooking time.

2. For vinaigrette, in a screw-top jar combine the remaining oil, the vinegar, thyme, sugar, ¼ teaspoon salt, and ¼ teaspoon pepper; cover and shake to combine.

3. On four dinner plates, arrange chicken, cucumber ribbons, sliced tomatoes, and olives. If desired, sprinkle with feta cheese. Drizzle vinaigrette over salads.

FOR 8 SERVINGS Prepare using method above, except in Step 1 use 2 tablespoons oil. In Step 2 use ½ teaspoon each salt and pepper.

PER SERVING *336 cal., 23 g fat (3 g sat. fat), 73 mg chol., 569 mg sodium, 7 g carb., 2 g fiber, 25 g pro.*

Papaya and Coconut Chicken Salad

While this salad is still a bit of an indulgence, it is much lighter than deep-fried coconut chicken. As the chicken bakes, the coconut takes on a toasty brown color and flavor.

1. Preheat oven to 450°F. Line a baking sheet with foil; set aside. Cut chicken into strips. Sprinkle chicken with ½ teaspoon of the salt. Place coconut in a shallow dish. Roll chicken in coconut to coat, pressing lightly to adhere. Transfer to the prepared baking sheet. Bake about 12 minutes or until coconut is golden and chicken is no longer pink.

2. Meanwhile, peel, seed, and cut papaya in cubes. For dressing, place ¼ cup papaya cubes in blender or food processor; add vinegar, oil, honey, the remaining salt, and cayenne pepper. Blend or process until smooth. Toss ¼ cup of the dressing with greens; divide among four plates.

3. Top greens with chicken, remaining papaya, and blueberries. Pass remaining dressing.

FOR 8 SERVINGS Prepare using method above, except in Step 1 use 1 teaspoon of the salt. In Step 2 use ½ cup papaya cubes. Toss ½ cup of the dressing with the greens; divide among eight plates.

PER SERVING *526 cal., 30 g fat (15 g sat. fat), 66 mg chol., 639 mg sodium, 35 g carb., 6 g fiber, 30 g pro.*

PREP 20 minutes
BAKE 12 minutes at 450°F

4 servings	ingredients	8 servings
1 lb.	skinless, boneless chicken breast halves	2 lb.
¾ tsp.	salt	1½ tsp.
1½ cups	flaked coconut	3 cups
1	medium papaya	2
¼ cup	cider vinegar	½ cup
¼ cup	vegetable oil	½ cup
1 Tbsp.	honey	2 Tbsp.
dash	cayenne pepper	dash
1	5-oz. pkg. mixed salad greens	2
¾ cup	blueberries	1½

Open-Face Chicken Salad Sandwiches

This is not your mother's chicken salad sandwich. A vinaigrette-dressed salad is studded with grapes and fresh baby spinach and served—with a knife and fork—on top of a toasted, cheesy French baguette.

1. Preheat broiler. Line a 15×10×1-inch baking pan with foil; lightly brush with some olive oil. Place chicken and grapes in a single layer in pan; drizzle remaining oil, then lightly sprinkle with salt and pepper. Broil 2 to 3 inches from heat for 10 minutes or until chicken is cooked through and begins to brown.

2. For chicken salad, in a large bowl toss together spinach, cooked chicken, grapes, any pan juices, and vinegar.

3. Cut baguette into 4 portions, slice nearly through, place open on the baking sheet, then top with cheese. Broil 2 to 3 minutes to melt cheese. Layer open baguettes with chicken salad. Drizzle with any remaining dressing in bowl. Top with freshly ground black pepper.

PER SERVING *822 cal., 32 g fat (10 g sat. fat), 60 mg chol., 1,646 mg sodium, 96 g carb., 7 g fiber, 38 g pro.*

START TO FINISH **25 minutes**

4 servings	ingredients	8 servings
2 Tbsp.	olive oil	¼ cup
14 oz.	chicken tenders	28 oz.
2 cups	seedless red grapes, whole and/or halved	4 cups
	Salt and freshly ground black pepper	
6 cups	fresh baby spinach	12 cups
2 Tbsp.	red wine vinegar	¼ cup
1	baguette-style French bread	2
4 oz.	provolone cheese, thinly sliced	8 oz.

Honey-Nut Chicken Salad with Citrus and Feta

A refreshing change of pace from traditional mayo-based chicken salad, this melange of chicken, feta cheese, dried apricots, and toasted hazelnuts is cloaked in a creamy dressing of Greek yogurt, honey, fresh mint, and orange peel.

1. For dressing, in a medium bowl combine yogurt, honey, snipped mint, orange peel, salt, and pepper. If necessary, stir in milk, 1 tablespoon at a time, to reach desired consistency.

2. In an extra-large bowl combine chicken, feta cheese, quartered apricots, and hazelnuts. Add dressing; stir gently to coat. If desired, cover and chill for up to 2 hours.

3. Serve salad on a serving platter with lettuce leaves. If desired, garnish with additional feta cheese, dried apricots, hazelnuts, and mint sprigs.

*__*TIP__ To toast hazelnuts, preheat oven to 350°F. Spread nuts in a single layer in a shallow baking pan. Bake for 8 to 10 minutes or until lightly toasted, stirring once to toast evenly. Cool nuts slightly. Place the warm nuts on a clean kitchen towel; rub with the towel to remove the loose skins.*

PER SERVING *687 cal., 27 g fat (11 g sat. fat), 148 mg chol., 714 mg sodium, 54 g carb., 4 g fiber, 57 g pro.*

START TO FINISH **40 minutes**

4 servings	ingredients	8 servings
2 cups	plain Greek yogurt	4 cups
½ cup	honey	1 cup
2 Tbsp.	snipped fresh mint	¼ cup
1 tsp.	finely shredded orange peel	2 tsp.
½ tsp.	salt	1 tsp.
¼ tsp.	black pepper	½ tsp.
1 Tbsp.	milk (optional)	2 Tbsp.
1½ lb. (3 cups)	cooked chicken breast, cut into 1-inch pieces	3 lb. (6 cups)
½ cup (2 oz.)	crumbled feta cheese	1 cup (4 oz.)
½ cup	quartered dried apricots	1 cup
½ cup	coarsely chopped hazelnuts (filberts), toasted*	1 cup
	Lettuce leaves	
	Crumbled feta cheese (optional)	
	Dried apricots (optional)	
	Toasted hazelnuts* (filberts) (optional)	
	Fresh mint sprigs (optional)	

CHAPTER 3

Meat

Satisfy hearty appetites with these steaks, burgers, chops, roasts, and sausages.

76

80

100

Quick Paprika Steaks with Tomato Gravy

Substitute smoked paprika for the standard sweet paprika to add a nice smoky flavor to these skillet-cooked steaks.

START TO FINISH **25 minutes**

4 servings	ingredients	8 servings
¼ cup	all-purpose flour	½ cup
1 tsp.	paprika	2 tsp.
½ tsp.	salt	1 tsp.
¼ tsp.	black pepper	½ tsp.
4	4-oz. beef breakfast or skillet steaks, about ½ inch thick	8
3 Tbsp.	olive oil	6 Tbsp.
2 oz.	queso fresco or Monterey Jack cheese, thinly sliced	4 oz.
6	medium tomatoes, seeded and cut up	12
6	cloves garlic, chopped	12
1 to 2 Tbsp.	snipped fresh sage	3 to 4 Tbsp.
¼ tsp.	salt	½ tsp.
½ tsp.	black pepper	1 tsp.
	Arugula (optional)	

1. For steaks, in a shallow dish combine flour, paprika, the ½ teaspoon salt, and ¼ teaspoon pepper. Dredge steaks in flour mixture (reserve any remaining flour mixture). In an extra-large skillet heat 1 tablespoon of the oil over medium-high heat. Reduce heat to medium. Cook steaks, uncovered, in hot oil for 4 to 5 minutes per side or until medium doneness (160°F); top with cheese the last 2 minutes of cooking. Remove steaks from skillet; keep warm.

2. While steaks are cooking, place tomatoes in a food processor. Cover and pulse with several on-off turns until tomatoes are coarsely chopped.

3. For tomato gravy, in the same skillet heat the remaining 2 tablespoons olive oil over medium heat. Add garlic; cook and stir about 1 minute or until garlic is golden. Stir in the tomatoes, sage, the ¼ teaspoon salt, the ½ teaspoon pepper, and any remaining flour mixture. Bring to boiling; reduce heat. Simmer, uncovered, about 5 minutes or until desired consistency. If desired, place a small handful of arugula on each plate. Place steaks on plates. Spoon some of the tomato gravy over steaks; pass remaining gravy.

FOR 8 SERVINGS Prepare using method above, except in Step 1 use 1 teaspoon salt and ½ teaspoon pepper and 2 tablespoons of the oil. In Step 3 heat the remaining 4 tablespoons oil; use ½ teaspoon salt and 1 teaspoon pepper.

PER SERVING *365 cal., 21 g fat (6 g sat. fat), 77 mg chol., 615 mg sodium, 16 g carb., 3 g fiber, 29 g pro.*

Frizzled Eggs over Garlic Steak and Mushroom Hash

If you love garlic, you will love this anytime dish of a crisp-cooked fried egg and breakfast steak over hash browns topped with a generous dose of toasty garlic slices.

1. In a very large skillet heat 1 tablespoon of the oil. Cook potatoes and mushrooms, covered, over medium-high heat for 10 minutes. Stir occasionally. Remove from skillet; cover to keep warm.

2. Sprinkle steaks with salt and pepper. Heat remaining oil in skillet. Cook steaks and garlic for 3 to 4 minutes, turning once, until desired doneness. Remove from skillet; cover to keep warm.

3. Add eggs to the hot skillet; sprinkle with salt and pepper. Cook to desired doneness. Place potatoes, steaks, and eggs on plates. If desired, sprinkle with snipped fresh tarragon.

FOR 8 SERVINGS Prepare using method above, except in Step 1 use 2 tablespoons oil.

PER SERVING *324 cal., 15 g fat (3 g sat. fat), 258 mg chol., 397 mg sodium, 17 g carb., 2 g fiber, 29 g pro.*

START TO FINISH **30 minutes**

4 servings	ingredients	8 servings
2 Tbsp.	vegetable oil	¼ cup
2 cups	frozen diced hash brown potatoes with onions and peppers	4 cups
1	8-oz. pkg. sliced fresh mushrooms	2
4	3- to 4-oz. thin breakfast steaks	8
	Salt	
	Black pepper	
4 to 6	cloves garlic, thinly sliced	10 to 12
4	eggs	8

Beef and Baby Spuds with Tomato-Olive Ragout

START TO FINISH 25 minutes

4 servings	ingredients	8 servings
1 lb.	baby Yukon gold or new potatoes, halved and/or quartered	2 lb.
4	4-oz. beef steaks, ½ inch thick (flat iron, strip, sirloin, or ribeye)	8
	Salt and black pepper	
4 tsp.	olive oil	8 tsp.
8 oz.	cherry tomatoes	1 lb.
3	cloves garlic, sliced	6
¾ cup	pitted green olives, coarsely chopped	1½ cups
1 tsp.	snipped fresh oregano*	2 tsp.

If you can find it, try a flat iron steak in this dish. It's a relatively new cut that is prized for its flavor and tenderness in comparison to its price and relative leanness.

1. Cook potatoes, covered with vented plastic wrap, in a microwave-safe bowl for 5 minutes, stirring once.

2. Meanwhile, season steaks with salt and pepper. Heat an extra-large skillet over medium-high heat; add 1 teaspoon of the oil. Add steaks; cook 3 to 4 minutes per side. Transfer to platter; cover. In the same skillet cook tomatoes and garlic in 1 teaspoon oil until softened. Stir in olives and oregano; cook 3 minutes more.

3. In a separate nonstick skillet cook potatoes in 2 teaspoons hot oil for 4 minutes over medium-high heat. Season with salt and pepper. Serve steaks and potatoes with sauce.

FOR 8 SERVINGS Prepare using method above, except in Step 2 use 2 teaspoons of the oil to cook the steaks and 2 teaspoons of the oil to cook the tomatoes and garlic. In Step 3 cook potatoes in 4 teaspoons hot oil.

*TIP If desired, for 4 servings, use ½ teaspoon dried oregano, crushed, for the 1 teaspoon snipped fresh oregano. For 8 servings, use 1 teaspoon dried oregano, crushed, for the 2 teaspoons snipped fresh oregano.

PER SERVING *409 cal., 23 g fat (7 g sat. fat), 53 mg chol., 643 mg sodium, 24 g carb., 4 g fiber, 26 g pro.*

Five-Spice Beef Kabobs

Five-spice powder is a spice blend that is used extensively in Chinese cooking. It usually contains equal parts cinnamon, cloves, fennel seeds, star anise, and Szechwan peppercorns.

1. Thinly slice steak across grain. If necessary, flatten slices with palm of hand or meat mallet to ¼-inch thickness. In a medium bowl combine beef, soy sauce, and five-spice powder; toss to coat beef. Thread beef on skewers.*

2. For a charcoal or gas grill, place kabobs on grill rack directly over medium heat. Cover and grill for 4 to 6 minutes or to desired doneness, turning once halfway through grilling.

3. Meanwhile, in a small bowl combine yogurt and snipped mint. From one lime, finely shred 1 teaspoon peel. Juice the lime. Stir peel and 1 tablespoon juice into yogurt. Cut remaining lime in wedges if desired.

4. Serve kabobs with yogurt sauce and lime wedges. Top with additional fresh mint.

FOR 8 SERVINGS Prepare using method above, except in Step 3 use 2 teaspoons finely shredded lime peel and 2 tablespoons lime juice.

***TIP** If using wooden skewers, soak in water 30 minutes before grilling.

TIP To serve with fresh carrot ribbons, use a vegetable peeler to cut thin ribbons. Toss with a squeeze of lime juice and lightly sprinkle with five-spice powder.

PER SERVING *213 cal., 8 g fat (3 g sat. fat), 74 mg chol., 366 mg sodium, 5 g carb., 1 g fiber, 29 g pro.*

START TO FINISH **20 minutes**

4 servings	ingredients	8 servings
1 lb.	beef flank steak or boneless beef sirloin	2 lb.
2 Tbsp.	reduced-sodium soy sauce	¼ cup
1 to 1½ tsp.	Chinese five-spice powder	2½ to 3 tsp.
1	6-oz. carton plain Greek yogurt	2
1 Tbsp.	snipped fresh mint leaves	2 Tbsp.
2	small limes	4
	Fresh mint leaves	

Peach-Horseradish-Sauced Ribeyes

PREP 10 minutes
GRILL 11 minutes

4 servings	ingredients	8 servings
2 (1½ lb. total)	beef ribeye steaks, cut 1 inch thick	4 (3 lb. total)
1 Tbsp.	olive oil	2 Tbsp.
1 Tbsp.	steak seasoning	2 Tbsp.
⅓ cup	peach preserves	⅔ cup
2 Tbsp.	prepared horseradish	¼ cup
2 Tbsp.	bottled plum sauce	¼ cup
	Grilled peaches (optional)*	

If you decide to add the grilled peaches to the platter, make this hearty dish in August—the peak of peach season—when the fruit is at its sweet and juicy best.

1. Trim fat from steaks. Brush steaks with oil; sprinkle with steak seasoning. For a charcoal or gas grill, place steaks directly on the grill rack over medium heat. Cover and grill for 10 to 12 minutes for medium-rare (145°F) or 12 to 15 minutes for medium (160°F), turning once halfway through grilling. Remove from grill.

2. Meanwhile, for Peach-Horseradish Sauce, in a small bowl stir together preserves, horseradish, and plum sauce. Slice steaks. Serve with sauce and, if desired, grilled peaches.

*TIP To grill peaches, halve and pit peaches. Grill on rack of uncovered grill directly over medium heat for 8 to 10 minutes or until tender and lightly browned, turning once.

PER SERVING *399 cal., 18 g fat (6 g sat. fat), 100 mg chol., 700 mg sodium, 23 g carb., 1 g fiber, 35 g pro.*

Beef and Noodle Toss

This tasty dish is a great way to use up leftover dried lasagna noodles—particularly if you have a just a few in several different boxes.

1. Break noodles in half. In a large pot cook noodles according to package directions. Drain but do not rinse.

2. Meanwhile, sprinkle beef with salt and pepper; toss with flour. In an extra-large skillet heat oil over medium-high heat. Add meat, any remaining flour, and the tomatoes to the skillet. Cook for 3 to 4 minutes or until beef is well browned, stirring frequently. Add mushrooms and garlic to meat in skillet. Cook for 5 to 6 minutes more. Add beef broth; cook for 3 to 4 minutes more or until beef is done, mushrooms are tender, and liquid is slightly thickened.

3. Add cooked noodles to skillet; stir gently to coat. Heat through. Serve in pasta or soup bowls.

PER SERVING *468 cal., 16 g fat (5 g sat. fat), 40 mg chol., 712 mg sodium, 52 g carb., 3 g fiber, 28 g pro.*

START TO FINISH **25 minutes**

4 servings	ingredients	8 servings
8 oz.	dried lasagna noodles	1 lb.
12 oz.	boneless beef sirloin, cut into bite-size pieces	24 oz.
½ tsp.	salt	1 tsp.
½ tsp.	black pepper	1 tsp.
2 Tbsp.	all-purpose flour	¼ cup
1 Tbsp.	olive oil	2 Tbsp.
2 cups	grape tomatoes	4 cups
8 oz.	sliced cremini or button mushrooms	1 lb.
4	cloves garlic, minced	8
1	14.5-oz. can beef broth	2

Open-Face Italian Beef Sandwiches

Precooked Italian-style beef roast is embellished with vinegar, sugar, black pepper, and sweet peppers for flavor that tastes like it cooked all day.

4 servings	ingredients	8 servings
¼ cup	white wine vinegar or cider vinegar	½ cup
1 tsp.	sugar	2 tsp.
½ tsp.	black pepper	1 tsp.
1	17-oz. pkg. refrigerated Italian-style herbed cooked beef roast au jus, undrained	2
1 cup	sliced baby or regular-size red or yellow sweet peppers	2 cups
2	square whole grain ciabatta rolls or buns	4
4 slices	provolone cheese	8 slices
2 Tbsp.	snipped fresh parsley	¼ cup
	Snipped fresh parsley	

1. Preheat broiler. In a large microwave-safe bowl combine vinegar, sugar, and black pepper. Add beef and sweet peppers. Cover and cook on high for 4 minutes.

2. Meanwhile, split rolls and place, cut sides up, on a baking sheet. Broil 3 to 4 inches from heat for 1 minute or until lightly toasted. Top each roll with cheese; broil 1 to 2 minutes until cheese is melted.

3. Using a fork, coarsely shred beef. Stir in parsley. With a slotted spoon, mound beef mixture onto rolls. Sprinkle with additional snipped parsley. Serve with any remaining cooking liquid.

PER SERVING *341 cal., 15 g fat (8 g sat. fat), 78 mg chol., 774 mg sodium, 22 g carb., 2 g fiber, 31 g pro.*

Roast Beef Quesadillas

The double-decker effect of these quesadillas is created by folding the filled tortillas in half and then in half again. Rather than being part of the filling, the cheese is sprinkled on top before broiling to create a melty, toasty crust.

1. Preheat broiler. In a large skillet combine beef in its juices, salsa, and peppers. Cook, covered, over medium heat for 10 minutes, stirring occasionally to break up beef.

2. Spray a baking sheet with cooking spray. For quesadillas, spoon some of the beef mixture on half of each tortilla. Fold tortillas over meat, then fold in quarters. Place tortillas on prepared sheet. Sprinkle cheese on each tortilla. Broil for 1 to 2 minutes or until cheese is melted and tortillas begin to crisp. Sprinkle with cilantro.

PER SERVING *428 cal., 18 g fat (9 g sat. fat), 86 mg chol., 983 mg sodium, 34 g carb., 3 g fiber, 34 g pro.*

START TO FINISH **25 minutes**

4 servings	ingredients	8 servings
1	17-oz. pkg. refrigerated cooked beef roast au jus	2
¾ cup	bottled chunky salsa	1½ cups
2	sweet yellow peppers, thinly sliced	4
2	fresh jalapeños, seeded and sliced (see tip, page 10)	4
4	10-inch flour tortillas	8
	Nonstick cooking spray	
¾ cup	shredded cheddar cheese	1½ cups
	Fresh cilantro (optional)	

Meat Loaf Muffins

Serve these mini meat loaves with whole wheat dinner rolls and a side of green beans.

PREP 40 minutes
BAKE 45 minutes at 350°F
STAND 10 minutes

6 servings	ingredients	12 servings
1	egg, lightly beaten	2
¼ cup	seasoned fine dry bread crumbs	½ cup
¼ cup	finely chopped fresh mushrooms	½ cup
¼ cup	shredded carrot	½ cup
3 Tbsp.	chopped onion	⅓ cup
4 tsp.	ketchup	3 Tbsp.
1½ tsp.	Dijon mustard	1 Tbsp.
1½ tsp.	Worcestershire sauce	1 Tbsp.
1	clove garlic, minced	2
1 lb.	lean ground beef	2 lb.
¼ cup	ketchup	½ cup
2 Tbsp.	whole cranberry sauce	¼ cup
½ tsp.	chili powder	1 tsp.
½	24-oz. pkg. refrigerated sour cream and chive mashed potatoes	1
¼ cup (1 oz.)	shredded cheddar or Parmesan cheese	½ cup (2 oz.)
	Snipped fresh chives (optional)	

1. Preheat oven to 350°F. In a large bowl stir together egg, bread crumbs, mushrooms, carrot, onion, the 4 teaspoons ketchup, mustard, Worcestershire sauce, and garlic. Add ground beef; mix well.

2. Lightly press about ⅓ cup of the meat mixture into each of six 2½-inch muffin cups. Place muffin pan on a large baking sheet. In a small bowl stir together the ¼ cup ketchup, cranberry sauce, and chili powder. Top each meat portion with 1 tablespoon of the ketchup mixture.

3. Bake, uncovered, about 40 minutes or until internal temperature registers 160°F on an instant-read thermometer.

4. Meanwhile, heat potatoes according to package directions. Using a ¼-cup ice cream scoop, top each muffin with potatoes. Sprinkle potatoes evenly with cheese. Return to oven and bake, uncovered, about 5 minutes or until cheese is melted.

5. Let muffins stand in pan on a wire rack for 10 minutes. Using a slotted spoon, transfer muffins to a serving platter. If desired, sprinkle tops with snipped fresh chives.

FOR 12 SERVINGS Prepare using method above, except in Step 1 use 3 tablespoons ketchup. In Step 2 use twelve 2½-inch muffin cups and ½ cup ketchup.

PER SERVING *310 cal., 18 g fat (8 g sat. fat), 100 mg chol., 603 mg sodium, 18 g carb., 1 g fiber, 19 g pro.*

Pork Cutlets with Brussels Sprouts

Those who think they don't like Brussels sprouts will be more than pleasantly surprised by the effect pan-frying in hot butter has on the tiny green globes. They get crisp and caramelized and completely delicious—a perfect pairing with the pork and sour cream sauce.

1. Using a meat mallet or heavy rolling pin, pound pork, layered between plastic wrap, to ¼-inch thickness. In a shallow dish combine flour, half the paprika, salt, and pepper. Coat pork in flour mixture; set aside.

2. In a large skillet cook sprouts in hot butter over medium-high heat for 5 to 8 minutes, until crisp-tender and edges are brown. Remove from skillet. Cover and keep warm.

3. In the same skillet add additional butter if needed. Cook pork 4 to 5 minutes, turning once, until golden outside and slightly pink in center. Remove from skillet. Cover; keep warm.

4. For sauce, combine sour cream, milk, and brown sugar. Whisk into skillet. Heat through (do not boil). Serve sauce, sprinkled with remaining paprika, over pork and sprouts.

PER SERVING *395 cal., 22 g fat (11 g sat. fat), 108 mg chol., 480 mg sodium, 22 g carb., 5 g fiber, 29 g pro.*

START TO FINISH **28 minutes**

4 servings	ingredients	8 servings
4	½-inch-thick boneless pork chops	8
¼ cup	all-purpose flour	½ cup
2 tsp.	paprika or smoked paprika	4 tsp.
½ tsp.	salt	1 tsp.
½ tsp.	black pepper	1 tsp.
1 lb.	Brussels sprouts, trimmed and halved	2 lb.
2 Tbsp.	butter	4 Tbsp.
1	8-oz. carton light sour cream	2
2 Tbsp.	milk or half-and-half	¼ cup
1 tsp.	packed brown sugar	2 tsp.

Lemon-Sage Pork Chops on a Stick

PREP 20 minutes
MARINATE 4 hours
GRILL 7 minutes
STAND 3 minutes

6 servings	ingredients	12 servings
6	6-oz. boneless pork loin chops, cut 1-inch-thick	12
1½ tsp.	finely shredded lemon peel	1 Tbsp.
⅓ cup	lemon juice	¾ cup
⅓ cup	olive oil	¾ cup
3 Tbsp.	finely chopped shallot	⅓ cup
3 Tbsp.	coarse ground mustard	⅓ cup
2 Tbsp.	snipped fresh sage	¼ cup
3	cloves garlic, minced	6
1 tsp.	coarsely ground black pepper	2 tsp.
½ tsp.	salt	1 tsp.
6	8×¼-inch wooden skewers, dowels, or bamboo chopsticks (see tip, page 75)	12
	Snipped fresh sage (optional)	
	Lemon wedges (optional)	

Don't wait for the state fair to enjoy juicy grilled pork chops on a stick. When you need hearty food that is truly portable and fork-free, this is it.

1. Place chops in a resealable plastic bag set in a shallow dish. For marinade, in a small bowl whisk together lemon peel, lemon juice, olive oil, shallot, mustard, sage, garlic, pepper, and salt. Pour marinade over chops; seal bag. Marinate in the refrigerator for 4 to 6 hours, turning bag occasionally. Drain chops, discarding marinade. Insert a wooden chopstick into a short side of each chop.

2. For a charcoal or gas grill, place chops on the grill rack directly over medium heat. Cover and grill for 7 to 9 minutes or until chops are slightly pink in center and juices run clear (145°F), turning once halfway through grilling. Remove from grill; let chops rest for 3 minutes. If desired, sprinkle with additional fresh sage.

PER SERVING 449 cal., 33 g fat (10 g sat. fat), 102 mg chol., 309 mg sodium, 2 g carb., 0 g fiber, 34 g pro.

Pork Chops, Apples, and Greens

Some apple varieties hold their shape better than others when exposed to heat. In this dish, you want the apple slices to stay intact and not turn into applesauce. Good choices include Rome, Golden Delicious, Granny Smith, and Braeburn.

1. Place each chop between two sheets of waxed paper or plastic wrap. With the flat side of a meat mallet or rolling pin, pound pork to ½-inch thickness.

2. In a food processor process bread into crumbs; place in a shallow dish. In a second shallow dish lightly beat egg with half the salt. Dip pork into egg mixture, then into bread crumbs to coat.

3. In an extra-large skillet heat oil over medium heat. Add pork chops. Cook for 5 to 7 minutes or until golden on the outside and an instant-read thermometer inserted in the side of the pork registers (145°F), turning once halfway through cooking. Transfer chops to a platter; cover to keep warm.

4. Stir honey, mustard, and vinegar into drippings in skillet. Add apple slices; cook and stir about 3 minutes or until crisp-tender. Toss in spinach to barely wilt; sprinkle with the remaining salt.

5. Serve chops with apples and spinach. Drizzle with pan juices and sprinkle with pepper.

PER SERVING *446 cal., 21 g fat (6 g sat. fat), 150 mg chol., 700 mg sodium, 26 g carb., 5 g fiber, 35 g pro.*

START TO FINISH **30 minutes**

4 servings	ingredients	8 servings
4	5-oz. boneless pork chops	8
3 slices	day-old bread, torn into pieces	6 slices
1	egg	2
½ tsp.	salt	1 tsp.
2 Tbsp.	olive oil	¼ cup
¼ cup	honey	½ cup
2 Tbsp.	spicy brown mustard	¼ cup
2 Tbsp.	cider vinegar	¼ cup
2 medium	cooking apples, cored and sliced	4 medium
6 cups	packaged baby spinach	12 cups
	Freshly ground black pepper	

Mustard-Glazed Pork Chops

The pungent flavor of mustard complements the sweetness of pork in a particularly wonderful way. Use almost any kind of mustard you like in this recipe except for the ballpark-yellow variety.

1. Season pork with salt and pepper. In an extra-large large skillet heat olive oil over medium-high heat. Add pork and onion to skillet. Cook for 3 minutes; turn pork and onions. Cook for 3 minutes more.

2. Meanwhile, in a small microwave-safe bowl combine preserves, mustard, the water, paprika, and nutmeg. Heat on high for 1 to 2 minutes or until melted. Pour over pork in skillet. Reduce heat to medium. Cook, covered, for 5 minutes or until pork is cooked through (145°F).

3. Divide pork and onion mixture among serving plates. If desired, top with sage.

PER SERVING *503 cal., 32 g fat (11 g sat. fat), 89 mg chol., 313 mg sodium, 31 g carb., 1 g fiber, 20 g pro.*

START TO FINISH **25 minutes**

4 servings	ingredients	8 servings
4	½-inch-thick bone-in pork chops	8
	Salt	
	Black pepper	
2 tsp.	olive oil	4 tsp.
1	large onion, cut into thin wedges	2
½ cup	apricot preserves	1 cup
1 Tbsp.	Dijon or spicy mustard	2 Tbsp.
¼ cup	water	½ cup
1 tsp.	paprika	2 tsp.
½ tsp.	ground nutmeg	1 tsp.
	Fresh sage leaves (optional)	

Pecan-Crusted Pork with Orange-Maple Glaze

Be sure to use pure maple syrup in this recipe, even if you don't routinely put it on your pancakes. It is pricey, but it is a relatively small amount—and the flavor and consistency of the sauce depends upon it.

1. Trim pork, then cut into ½-inch slices. Flatten slices with palm of hand; season pork with salt and pepper.

2. Place 3 tablespoons of the syrup in a shallow dish; place pecans in a second shallow dish. In an extra-large skillet heat oil over medium heat. Coat pork in syrup, then press in pecans. Place pork in skillet in single layer; top with remaining pecans and syrup from dish. Cook 3 to 4 minutes or until juices run clear, turning once. Remove from skillet. With a slotted spoon, remove any pecan pieces in skillet; spoon over pork.

3. Juice one of the oranges. Stir orange juice, the remaining 1 tablespoon maple syrup, cumin, and cayenne into skillet. Cook, uncovered, for 1 to 2 minutes until slightly thickened. Pour over pork. Cut remaining orange into wedges; serve pork with orange wedges.

FOR 8 SERVINGS Prepare using method above, except in Step 2 use 6 tablespoons of the maple syrup. In Step 3 juice two oranges; use remaining 2 tablespoons syrup; cut remaining oranges into wedges.

PER SERVING *537 cal., 33 g fat (4 g sat. fat), 111 mg chol., 381 mg sodium, 25 g carb., 4 g fiber, 38 g pro.*

START TO FINISH **30 minutes**

4 servings	ingredients	8 servings
1½ lb.	pork tenderloin	3 lb.
½ tsp.	salt	1 tsp.
¼ tsp.	black pepper	½ tsp.
¼ cup	pure maple syrup	½ cup
1 cup	pecan pieces, finely chopped	2 cups
2 Tbsp.	vegetable oil	¼ cup
2	oranges	4
¼ tsp.	ground cumin	½ tsp.
¼ tsp.	cayenne pepper	½ tsp.

Caramelized Pork with Melon

To get the best cantaloupe, check for ripeness: It should smell sweet and slightly musky and should be free of bruises or indentations. It should feel heavy for its size, and the stem end should yield just slightly when pressed.

4 servings	ingredients	8 servings
1	small cantaloupe	2
¼ cup	orange juice	½ cup
3 Tbsp.	hoisin sauce	6 Tbsp.
4	pork loin rib chops, cut ½ inch thick	8
	Salt and black pepper	
1 Tbsp.	vegetable oil	2 Tbsp.
3	green onions, thinly sliced	6
	Napa cabbage (optional)	

1. Remove rind and seeds from cantaloupe; chop. In a food processor or blender combine 2 cups of the chopped melon and orange juice. Cover and process or blend until smooth. Transfer ½ cup of the pureed melon to a small bowl; stir in hoisin sauce. Strain remaining puree and reserve the juice; discard solids.

2. Lightly sprinkle chops with salt and pepper; brush generously with some of the melon mixture. In an extra-large skillet heat oil over medium-high heat. Add chops to skillet; cook for 6 to 8 minutes or until well browned and only a trace of pink remains (145°F), turning once. Remove chops from skillet.

3. Meanwhile, combine the remaining chopped melon, the strained juice, and the green onions; set aside.

4. For sauce, add the remaining melon mixture to skillet; cook and stir until heated through. Spoon sauce onto serving plates. Top each with a chop. Add chopped melon mixture to skillet to warm slightly; spoon over chops. If desired, serve with napa cabbage.

FOR 8 SERVINGS Prepare using method above, except in Step 1 use 4 cups of the chopped melon. Transfer 1 cup of the pureed melon to a small bowl.

PER SERVING *327 cal., 10 g fat (2 g sat. fat), 117 mg chol., 452 mg sodium, 19 g carb., 2 g fiber, 39 g pro.*

Pulled Pork Sandwiches with Root Beer Barbecue Sauce

Make this slow cooker pulled pork on a busy day when you need to feed a crowd at night. Everything goes in the cooker, and you can walk away for up to 10 hours. Make the sauce right before serving time.

1. Trim fat from meat. If necessary, cut roast to fit into cooker. Sprinkle meat with the salt and pepper. In a large skillet brown roast on all sides in hot oil. Drain. Transfer meat to a 4- to 5-quart slow cooker. Add onions, 1 cup of the root beer, and garlic. Cover; cook on low-heat setting for 8 to 10 hours or on high-heat setting for 4 to 5 hours.

2. Meanwhile, for sauce, in a medium saucepan combine the remaining root beer and bottled chili sauce. Bring to boiling; reduce heat.

3. Boil gently, uncovered, stirring occasionally, about 30 minutes or until root beer sauce is reduced to 2 cups. If desired, add bottled hot pepper sauce.

4. Transfer roast to a cutting board or serving platter. With a slotted spoon, remove onions from juices and place on serving platter. Discard juices. Using two forks, pull meat apart into shreds. To serve, line buns with lettuce leaves and tomato slices (if using). Add meat and onions; spoon on sauce.

FOR 16 SERVINGS Prepare using method above, except in Step 1 use a 6-quart slow cooker and 2 cups of the root beer. In Step 3 reduce root beer sauce to 4 cups.

PER SERVING *421 cal., 9 g fat (2 g sat. fat), 98 mg chol., 1,412 mg sodium, 48 g carb., 1 g fiber, 35 g pro.*

PREP **55 minutes**
SLOW COOK **8 hours (low) or 4 hours (high)**

8 servings	ingredients	16 servings
2½- to 3-lb.	boneless pork sirloin roast	5- to 6-lb.
½ tsp.	salt	1 tsp.
½ tsp.	black pepper	1 tsp.
1 Tbsp.	vegetable oil	2 Tbsp.
2	medium onions, cut into thin wedges	4
4 cups	root beer (do not use diet)	8 cups
2 Tbsp.	minced garlic	4 Tbsp.
1 cup	bottled chili sauce	2 cups
½ tsp.	hot pepper sauce (optional)	1 tsp.
8	hamburger buns or kaiser rolls, split and toasted	16
	Lettuce leaves (optional)	
	Tomato slices (optional)	

Italian Ravioli Casserole

Your slow cooker isn't just for making pot roast and other big pieces of meat This family-pleasing ravioli casserole is layered and cooked in the slow cooker while you go about your day. Serve with garlic bread and a crisp green salad.

1. Lightly coat the inside of a 3½- or 4-quart slow cooker with cooking spray;* set aside.

2. For sauce, in a Dutch oven cook sausage, ground beef, onion, and garlic until meat is brown and onion is tender, using a wooden spoon to break up meat as it cooks. Drain off fat. Stir pasta sauce, tomato sauce, and Italian seasoning into meat mixture in Dutch oven.

3. Place ½ cup of the meat mixture in the prepared cooker. Add half the frozen ravioli and sprinkle with ½ cup cheese. Top with half the remaining meat mixture. Add the remaining ravioli and ½ cup cheese. Top with the remaining meat mixture.

4. Cover and cook on low-heat setting for 4 hours. Turn off cooker. Sprinkle with the remaining cheese. Let stand, covered, for 15 minutes before serving.

FOR 10 SERVINGS Prepare using method above, except in Step 1 use a 6-quart slow cooker. In Step 3 add half the frozen ravioli and sprinkle with 1 cup cheese. Top with half the remaining meat mixture. Add the remaining ravioli and 1 cup cheese. Top with the remaining meat mixture. In Step 4 sprinkle with the remaining cheese.

***TIP** For easy cleanup, place a disposable slow cooker liner into slow cooker before adding the casserole ingredients. Follow the directions on the liner package.

PER SERVING *727 cal., 35 g fat (14 g sat. fat), 128 mg chol., 1,583 mg sodium, 67 g carb., 5 g fiber, 36 g pro.*

PREP 25 minutes
SLOW COOK 4 hours (low)
STAND 15 minutes

5 servings	ingredients	10 servings
	Nonstick cooking spray	
½ lb.	bulk Italian sausage	1 lb.
½ lb.	lean ground beef	1 lb.
½ cup	chopped onion	1 cup
1	clove garlic, minced	2
1	26- to 28-oz. jar sun-dried tomato pasta sauce	2
½	15-oz. can tomato sauce	1
½ tsp.	dried Italian seasoning, crushed	1 tsp.
1	25-oz. pkg. frozen cheese-filled ravioli	2
1¼ cups (5 oz.)	shredded Italian cheese blend	2½ cups (10 oz.)

Ginger Pork Rolls

Cucumber slices give these Asian-style sliders a refreshing crunch. Two generously stuffed rolls is a serving. At 433 calories and just 9 grams of fat, that seems like a very sweet deal.

START TO FINISH **30 minutes**

4 servings	ingredients	8 servings
1 cup	water	2 cups
⅔ cup	golden raisins	1⅓ cups
½ cup	coarsely chopped red onion	1 cup
3 Tbsp.	reduced-sodium soy sauce	6 Tbsp.
2 tsp.	ground ginger	4 tsp.
¼ tsp.	black pepper	½ tsp.
1 lb.	pork loin, thinly sliced into bite-size pieces	2 lb.
8	mini hamburger buns or dinner rolls, split	16
1	small cucumber, thinly sliced	2

1. In a large skillet combine the water, raisins, onion, soy sauce, and ginger. Bring to boiling; reduce heat. Simmer, covered, for 5 to 6 minutes or until raisins are plump and onion is tender. Using a slotted spoon, remove raisins and onion, reserving liquid in skillet. Place raisin and onions in a small bowl. Stir in pepper; set aside.

2. Add sliced pork to cooking liquid in skillet. Return to boiling; reduce heat. Simmer, uncovered, for 4 to 5 minutes or until pork is cooked through (just a trace of pink remains), turning once. Using the slotted spoon, remove pork slices.

3. Serve pork in buns with cucumber slices, raisins, and onion.

PER SERVING *433 cal., 9 g fat (2 g sat. fat), 74 mg chol., 797 mg sodium, 57 g carb., 3 g fiber, 34 g pro.*

Grilled Ham and Pineapple Burgers

The classic combination of ham and pineapple gets a modern twist in these fun burgers made of ground ham patties grilled and topped with grilled pineapple.

1. Snip enough basil to equal ⅓ cup. In a large bowl combine half the snipped basil and ground ham. Shape into four ¾-inch-thick patties.

2. For a charcoal or gas grill, place patties on the grill rack directly over medium heat for 14 to 18 minutes or until patties register 160°F with an instant-read thermometer, turning once halfway through grilling. Add pineapple to grill during last 6 minutes of grilling time, turning once.

3. Meanwhile, in a bowl combine mayonnaise, mustard, honey, and remaining snipped basil. Spread on cut sides of roll bottoms. Layer patties, remaining basil leaves, pineapple, and roll tops.

FOR 8 SERVINGS Prepare using method above, except in Step 1 snip enough basil to equal ⅔ cup. Shape patties into eight ¾-inch-thick patties.

*TIP For 4 servings substitute ½ pound each ground ham and ground pork for the 1 pound ground ham loaf. For 8 servings substitute 1 pound each ground ham and ground pork for the 2 pounds ground ham loaf.

PER SERVING 566 cal., 30 g fat (8 g sat. fat), 78 mg chol., 1,238 mg sodium, 49 g carb., 4 g fiber, 26 g pro.

START TO FINISH **30 minutes**

4 servings	ingredients	8 servings
2 cups	loosely packed fresh basil leaves	4 cups
1 lb.	ground ham loaf*	2 lb.
4	½-inch slices fresh pineapple	8
¼ cup	mayonnaise	½ cup
2 Tbsp.	yellow mustard	¼ cup
1 Tbsp.	honey	2 Tbsp.
4	kaiser rolls, split and toasted	8

Peppered Pork Burgers

With a generous dose of black pepper, paprika, garlic, and cumin, these grilled pork patties are not short on flavor.

1. For the honey-mustard spread, in a small bowl combine mayonnaise, mustard, and honey; cover and chill. In a medium bowl combine pork, black pepper, paprika, garlic powder, cumin, and salt. Shape into four ½-inch-thick patties.

2. For a charcoal or gas grill, place patties on the grill rack directly over medium heat. Cover and grill for 10 to 12 minutes or until an instant-read thermometer inserted into side of each patty registers 160°F, turning patties once halfway through grilling.

3. Spread honey-mustard spread on cut sides of bun tops. Place lettuce leaves, grilled patties, and roasted red peppers on bun bottoms. Add bun tops.

FOR 8 SERVINGS Prepare using method above, except in Step 1 shape patties into eight ½-inch-thick patties.

PER SERVING *272 cal., 8 g fat (2 g sat. fat), 63 mg chol., 510 mg sodium, 26 g carb., 3 g fiber, 23 g pro.*

PREP **20 minutes**
GRILL **10 minutes**

4 servings	ingredients	8 servings
3 Tbsp.	light mayonnaise	6 Tbsp.
1 Tbsp.	Dijon mustard	2 Tbsp.
1 tsp.	honey	2 tsp.
12 oz.	lean ground pork	24 oz.
½ tsp.	black pepper	1 tsp.
½ tsp.	paprika	1 tsp.
¼ tsp.	garlic powder	½ tsp.
¼ tsp.	ground cumin	½ tsp.
⅛ tsp.	salt	¼ tsp.
4	whole wheat hamburger buns, split and toasted	8
2	romaine lettuce leaves, halved	4
¾ cup	bottled roasted red sweet peppers, drained and divided into large pieces	1½ cups

Beer-Braised Brat Sandwiches

The bratwurst is first grilled for an infusion of smoke and charring, then braised in a flavorful mixture of beer, brown sugar, vinegar, caraway, thyme, and Worcestershire sauce. A cranberry-sweet pickle relish is the crowning touch.

1. Use the tines of a fork to pierce the skin of each bratwurst several times. For a charcoal grill, arrange medium-hot coals around a drip pan. Test for medium heat above pan. Place bratwurst on the grill rack over drip pan. Cover and grill for 20 to 25 minutes or until bratwurst are no longer pink and juices run clear (160°F), turning once halfway through grilling. (For a gas grill, preheat grill. Reduce heat to medium. Adjust for indirect cooking. Place bratwurst on grill rack over the burner that is turned off. Grill as directed.)

2. Meanwhile, in a Dutch oven cook onion in hot butter over medium heat about 5 minutes or until tender. Add beer, brown sugar, vinegar, caraway seeds, thyme, and Worcestershire sauce. Bring to boiling; reduce heat. Place bratwurst in beer mixture; keep warm until serving time.

3. For cranberry-pickle relish, in a small bowl combine the cranberry sauce and pickle relish.

4. Serve bratwurst in buns. Using a slotted spoon, top with some cooked onion slices and cranberry-pickle relish.

PER SERVING *682 cal., 33 g fat (12 g sat. fat), 76 mg chol., 1,341 mg sodium, 70 g carb., 3 g fiber, 20 g pro.*

PREP 30 minutes
GRILL 20 minutes

5 servings	ingredients	10 servings
5 (about 1¼ lb.)	uncooked bratwurst	10 (about 2½ lb.)
½	large onion, halved and cut into thin slices	1
2 Tbsp.	butter	¼ cup
1	12-oz. can dark German beer	2
1 Tbsp.	packed brown sugar	2 Tbsp.
1 Tbsp.	vinegar	2 Tbsp.
½ tsp.	caraway seeds	1 tsp.
½ tsp.	dried thyme, crushed	1 tsp.
½ tsp.	Worcestershire sauce	1 tsp.
½ cup	whole cranberry sauce	1 cup
¼ cup	sweet pickle relish	½ cup
5	hoagie buns, bratwursts buns, or other crusty rolls, split and toasted	10

Beer-Glazed Sausage and Apples

If you're trying to trim fat and calories, use a smoked sausage made from turkey or a blend of turkey and other meats.

1. In a large saucepan combine half the beer and the crushed red pepper; bring to boiling. Add sausage and green beans. Return to a simmer, cover and cook 5 to 8 minutes or until beans are tender. Drain. Set aside.

2. Meanwhile, in a large skillet melt half the butter; add apples. Cook, turning occasionally, just until apples are tender. Transfer to a platter.

3. Add sausage to skillet. Cook, turning occasionally, until browned on all sides. Add to platter; cover. Drain fat from skillet.

4. Carefully add remaining beer to skillet (mixture may foam); stir to scrape up browned bits. Add remaining butter, the brown sugar, cider vinegar, and orange peel. Bring to boiling; reduce heat and boil gently, uncovered, 5 to 6 minutes or until slightly thickened. Return sausage and green beans to skillet to glaze. Fold in apples. Return to serving platter. Sprinkle with sage.

PER SERVING *409 cal., 24 g fat (10 g sat. fat), 85 mg chol., 1,250 mg sodium, 31 g carb., 4 g fiber, 15 g pro.*

START TO FINISH **35 minutes**

4 servings	ingredients	8 servings
1	12-oz. bottle Belgium-style wheat beer	2
½ tsp.	crushed red pepper	1 tsp.
1	14- to 16-oz. pkg. smoked sausage, such as kielbasa, cut into 3-inch pieces	2
½ lb.	fresh green beans	1 lb.
2 Tbsp.	butter	4 Tbsp.
2	medium-size cooking apples, cored and thinly sliced	4
2 Tbsp.	packed brown sugar	¼ cup
1 Tbsp.	cider vinegar	2 Tbsp.
1 tsp.	finely shredded orange peel	2 tsp.
8	small sage leaves	16

Pork and Poblano Stew

The poblano chile is best-known in its cheese-stuffed and batter-fried state in a classic Mexican dish, chiles rellenos. It has a mild, slightly sweet (sometimes with a little heat) flavor that goes beautifully with pork in this Mexican-style stew.

1. In a medium bowl sprinkle chili powder over pork; toss to coat. In a large saucepan heat half the oil over medium-high heat. Cook the pork, about 4 minutes or until brown, stirring occasionally.

2. Add remaining oil to saucepan. Cook poblano pepper, sweet pepper, and onion in hot oil over medium-high heat about 5 minutes or just until vegetables are tender. Add tomatoes, broth, and cinnamon stick. Bring to boiling; reduce heat. Cover and simmer for 10 minutes. Uncover; stir in reserved pork and the orange juice. Simmer for 5 minutes more. Stir in orange peel.

3. Remove and discard stick cinnamon. Ladle stew into shallow bowls.

PER SERVING *300 cal., 11 g fat (2 g sat. fat), 87 mg chol., 534 mg sodium, 16 g carb., 4 g fiber, 32 g pro.*

PREP **15 minutes**
COOK **24 minutes**

4 servings	ingredients	8 servings
2 tsp.	hot chili powder	4 tsp.
1¼ lb.	pork tenderloin, cut into ¾- to 1-inch pieces	2½ lb.
2 Tbsp.	olive oil	¼ cup
1	fresh poblano pepper, seeded and cut into 1-inch pieces (see tip, page 10)	2
1	large red sweet pepper, seeded and cut into 1-inch pieces	2
1	medium onion, cut into thin wedges	2
1	14.5-oz. can fire-roasted tomatoes with garlic, undrained	2
1	14.5-oz. can reduced-sodium chicken broth	2
1	3-inch stick cinnamon	2
2 tsp.	finely shredded orange peel	4 tsp.
¼ cup	fresh orange juice	½ cup

Smoked Sausage Lasagna

This lasagna fuses Italian style with a splash of the unexpected—such as Monterey Jack cheese with jalapeño peppers in place of shredded mozzarella. Fennel, a crisp bulb with a licoricelike flavor, perfectly complements the smoky chicken sausage—whether you use sausage flavored with apple or the Italian-style variety.

1. Preheat oven to 350°F. Lightly coat a 2-quart baking dish with cooking spray; set aside. In a medium bowl stir together the pasta sauce and the olives. Spoon ⅓ cup of the sauce in prepared dish. Top with 2 lasagna noodles. In a small bowl stir together the ricotta cheese and 1 cup of the Monterey Jack cheese. Spoon half the mixture on the noodles in the dish. Sprinkle with 2 tablespoons of the Parmesan. Top with half the sausage and half the fennel. Spoon half the remaining sauce over the sausage layer.

2. Top with 2 more noodles, the remaining ricotta mixture, and the remaining sausage and fennel. Add 2 more noodles and the remaining sauce. Sprinkle with remaining Monterey Jack and Parmesan cheeses.

3. Cover with foil. Bake for 50 minutes. Let stand, covered, on a wire rack for 20 minutes before serving.

FOR 12 SERVINGS Prepare using method above, except in Step 1 use a 3-quart baking dish. Spoon ⅔ cup of the sauce in the prepared dish. Top with 4 lasagna noodles. In a bowl stir together 2 cups of the Monterey Jack cheese; spoon half onto the noodles and sprinkle with ¼ cup Parmesan cheese. In Step 2 top with 4 more noodles, the remaining ricotta mixture, remaining sausage and fennel. Add 4 more noodles and the remaining sauce. Sprinkle with remaining Monterey Jack and Parmesan cheeses.

PER SERVING *541 cal., 33 g fat (16 g sat. fat), 85 mg chol., 1,357 mg sodium, 29 g carb., 8 g fiber, 32 g pro.*

PREP **20 minutes**
BAKE **50 minutes at 350°F**
STAND **20 minutes**

6 servings	ingredients	12 servings
	Nonstick cooking spray	
2 cups	red pasta sauce, such as tomato-basil or roasted garlic and onion	4 cups
½ cup	pitted Kalamata olives, halved	1 cup
6	no-boil lasagna noodles	12
½	15-oz. container ricotta cheese	1
6 oz. (1½ cups)	Monterey Jack cheese with jalapeño peppers or Monterey Jack cheese, shredded	12 oz. (3 cups)
¼ cup	finely shredded Parmesan cheese	½ cup
8 oz.	smoked chicken sausage with apple or Italian sausage, halved lengthwise and sliced	1 lb.
1	medium fennel bulb, trimmed, halved lengthwise, and thinly sliced	2

CHAPTER 4

Seafood

Light and fresh fish and shellfish take on many forms and flavors in these recipes for salmon, tuna, whitefish, and sweet, succulent shrimp.

116

120

131

Fish Tacos with Lime Sauce

Shredded cabbage and carrot gives these fresh fish tacos topped with a creamy chili-lime mayo an irresistible crunch.

START TO FINISH **30 minutes**

4 servings	ingredients	8 servings
1 lb.	fresh or frozen tilapia or catfish fillets	2 lb.
3	limes	6
½ cup	mayonnaise	1 cup
1 tsp.	chili powder	2 tsp.
⅓ cup	all-purpose flour	⅔ cup
½ tsp.	salt	1 tsp.
2 Tbsp.	vegetable oil	¼ cup
8	taco shells or 6-inch flour tortillas, warmed	16
1 cup	shredded cabbage	2 cups
½ cup	shredded carrot	1 cup
1	fresh jalapeño or serrano chile pepper, thinly sliced (see tip, page 10)	2

1. Thaw fish, if frozen. Rinse fish; pat dry with paper towels. Cut fish into 1-inch pieces.

2. For sauce, juice two of the limes into a small bowl; cut the remaining lime into wedges and reserve for serving. Stir mayonnaise and chili powder into lime juice. Transfer ⅓ cup of the sauce to a medium bowl. Add fish; toss gently to coat.

3. In a shallow dish combine flour and salt. Dip fish in flour mixture to coat. In a large skillet heat oil over medium heat. Cook fish, about one-third at a time, in hot oil for 2 to 4 minutes or until fish flakes easily when tested with a fork, turning to brown evenly and adding more oil as necessary during cooking. Drain on paper towels.

4. Fill taco shells or tortillas with fish, cabbage, carrot, and jalapeño pepper. Serve with the remaining sauce and the reserved lime wedges.

FOR 8 SERVINGS Prepare using method above, except in Step 2 juice four of the limes; cut remaining two in wedges. Transfer ⅔ cup of the sauce to a medium bowl.

PER SERVING *652 cal., 39 g fat (5 g sat. fat), 67 mg chol., 557 mg sodium, 41 g carb., 2 g fiber, 31 g pro.*

Fish and Green Beans with Wasabi Mayonnaise

Meaty white cod is a great choice to use in this recipe that takes advantage of two Japanese ingredients—head-clearing wasabi horseradish and crispy panko bread crumbs.

1. Preheat oven to 450°F. Coat a baking pan with cooking spray; set aside. Shred peel and juice half the lime; cut remaining lime into wedges. Stir together juice, peel, wasabi paste, and mayonnaise. Transfer 1 tablespoon of the wasabi mayonnaise to a bowl. Cover and refrigerate remaining wasabi mayonnaise.

2. Sprinkle fish with salt. Place fish in baking pan. Coat with 1 tablespoon of the wasabi mayonnaise, then ¾ cup panko. Drizzle with melted butter. Bake on middle oven rack for 20 minutes or until fish flakes easily with a fork.

3. Remove fish from pan. Toss beans with panko remaining in baking pan. Sprinkle with remaining panko. Serve with remaining wasabi mayonnaise and lime wedges.

FOR 8 SERVINGS Prepare using method above, except in Step 1 transfer 2 tablespoons of the wasabi mayonnaise to a bowl. In Step 2 coat fish with 2 tablespoons of the wasabi mayonnaise, then 1½ cups panko.

PER SERVING *349 cal., 19 g fat (5 g sat. fat), 56 mg chol., 384 mg sodium, 18 g carb., 4 g fiber, 26 g pro.*

PREP **10 minutes**
BAKE **20 minutes at 450°F**

4 servings	ingredients	8 servings
	Nonstick cooking spray	
1	lime	2
1 to 3 tsp.	wasabi paste	3 to 6 tsp.
⅓ cup	mayonnaise	⅔ cup
1 to 1½ lb.	firm whitefish fillets, ½ inch thick, rinsed and dried	3 lb.
	Salt	
1 cup	panko bread crumbs	2 cups
1 Tbsp.	butter, melted	2 Tbsp.
12 oz.	tender young green beans, cooked	24 oz.
	Lime wedges	

Bacon, Egg, Spinach, and Tuna Salad

Slices of perfectly cooked tuna top this bacon, egg, and spinach salad drizzled with a warm honey-mustard vinaigrette. Take care not to overcook the tuna, which can easily dry out.

START TO FINISH 25 minutes

4 servings	ingredients	8 servings
4	eggs	8
6 slices	bacon slices	12 slices
12 oz.	tuna steaks	24 oz.
½ cup	white wine vinegar	1 cup
2 to 3 Tbsp.	honey	4 to 6 Tbsp.
1 Tbsp.	Dijon-style mustard	2 Tbsp.
1	6-oz. pkg. fresh baby spinach	2

1. Place eggs in a saucepan; cover with water. Bring to a rapid boil. Remove from heat; cover. Let stand 10 to 15 minutes (yolks will be soft-set at 10 minutes). Drain. Rinse with cold water; cool. Peel and quarter.

2. Meanwhile, in a large skillet cook bacon over medium heat until crisp. Drain reserving drippings in skillet. Crumble bacon and set aside. Remove 2 tablespoons drippings for dressing. Add tuna to skillet; cook over medium-high heat 3 minutes per side or until slightly pink in center. Transfer to a cutting board; cover and keep warm. Slice before serving.

3. Wipe skillet clean. Whisk in reserved drippings, vinegar, honey, and mustard to skillet. Bring to boiling.

4. Line plates with spinach. Top with sliced tuna, crumbled bacon, and egg wedges. Drizzle dressing and sprinkle pepper on each serving.

PER SERVING *481 cal., 32 g fat (10 g sat. fat), 289 mg chol., 702 mg sodium, 11 g carb., 1 g fiber, 34 g pro.*

Tuna Club Sandwiches with Roasted Pepper Sauce

A supersimple sauce made with bottled ranch dressing and jarred roasted red peppers gives these tuna salad sandwiches a special touch.

1. For the roasted red pepper sauce, in a blender container combine salad dressing and half the roasted red sweet peppers; process until nearly smooth.

2. For tuna filling, chop remaining peppers. In a bowl combine chopped peppers with tuna, corn, and ¼ cup of the roasted red pepper sauce.

3. For each club sandwich, spread two slices of toasted bread with tuna filling, layer with lettuce leaves, stack the two slices, then top with a third slice of toast. Cut in half diagonally. Serve with remaining roasted red pepper sauce.

FOR 8 SERVINGS Prepare using method above, except in Step 1 use ½ cup of the roasted red pepper sauce.

PER SERVING *401 cal., 18 g fat (2 g sat. fat), 41 mg chol., 1,020 mg sodium, 47 g carb., 1 g fiber, 29 g pro.*

START TO FINISH **25 minutes**

4 servings	ingredients	8 servings
⅓ cup	bottled ranch salad dressing	⅔ cup
½ cup	bottled roasted red sweet peppers, drained	1 cup
1	12-oz. can solid white tuna, drained and broken in chunks	2
1	8.75-oz. can whole kernel corn, drained	2
12	extra-thin slices sandwich bread, toasted	24
	Butterhead lettuce leaves	

Sesame-Ginger Grilled Salmon

PREP 15 minutes
MARINATE 2 hours
GRILL 7 minutes

4 servings	ingredients	8 servings
4	5-oz. fresh or frozen skinless salmon fillets	8
¼ cup	reduced-sodium soy sauce	½ cup
2 Tbsp.	lime juice	¼ cup
1 Tbsp.	grated fresh ginger	2 Tbsp.
½ tsp.	toasted sesame oil	1 tsp.
2 Tbsp.	sesame seeds, toasted (see tip, page 28)	¼ cup
	Lime wedges (optional)	
	Sliced green onion (optional)	

Serve this Asian-style salmon with hot cooked jasmine rice and a simple slaw (you can use packaged shredded coleslaw mix) tossed with bottled sesame-ginger or teriyaki dressing.

1. Thaw fish, if frozen. Rinse fish; pat dry with paper towels. Measure thickness of fish. Place fish in a shallow dish. For marinade, in a small bowl combine soy sauce, lime juice, ginger, and sesame oil. Pour marinade over fish; turn to coat. Cover and marinate in the refrigerator for 2 hours, turning fish occasionally. Drain fish, discarding marinade.

2. For a charcoal grill, arrange medium-hot coals around a drip pan. Test for medium heat above pan. Place fish on a greased grill rack over drip pan, tucking under any thin edges of fish. Sprinkle fish with toasted sesame seeds. Cover and grill for 7 to 9 minutes per ½-inch thickness of fish or until fish flakes easily when tested with a fork. (For a gas grill, preheat grill. Reduce heat to medium. Adjust for indirect cooking. Grill as above.) If desired, serve with lime wedges and sprinkle with sliced green onion.

PER SERVING *287 cal., 18 g fat (3 g sat. fat), 83 mg chol., 229 mg sodium, 1 g carb., 0 g fiber, 30 g pro.*

Simple Grilled Salmon with Kalamata-Orange Relish

The combination of salty, briny olives with the sweetness and acidity of oranges is heavenly on rich-tasting salmon.

1. Lightly grease a grill pan. Heat grill pan over medium heat. Brush salmon with 1 tablespoon of the oil. Sprinkle with smoked paprika, salt, and pepper. Place salmon on grill pan. Cook 4 to 6 minutes per ½-inch thickness of fish or until fish flakes when tested with a fork, turning once halfway through grilling.

2. Meanwhile, for relish, finely shred 1 teaspoon of peel from one of the oranges. Peel and dice oranges. In a medium bowl combine oranges, orange peel, olives, red sweet pepper, and remaining olive oil. Serve salmon with relish.

FOR 8 SERVINGS Prepare using method above, except in Step 1 brush salmon with 2 tablespoons of the oil. In Step 2 finely shred 2 teaspoons of the peel from the oranges.

PER SERVING *493 cal., 32 g fat (6 g sat. fat), 94 mg chol., 580 mg sodium, 15 g carb., 4 g fiber, 36 g pro.*

START TO FINISH **30 minutes**

4 servings	ingredients	8 servings
4	6-oz. skinless salmon fillets	8
2 Tbsp.	olive oil	¼ cup
1 tsp.	smoked paprika	2 tsp.
	Salt and black pepper	
3	medium oranges	6
½ cup	pitted Kalamata olives, coarsely chopped	1 cup
½ cup	chopped red sweet pepper	1 cup

Herbed Salmon

The simplest preparation for salmon—just lemon, fresh herbs, and butter—is sometimes best. Serve with a green salad and steamed new potatoes.

1. Preheat oven to 350°F. Rinse fish; pat dry. Cut into four equal pieces. Shred 1 teaspoon of peel from lemon; set aside. Cut lemon in half; juice half the lemon. In a small bowl combine lemon peel, snipped herbs, salt, pepper, and butter; stir to combine. Spread evenly on the salmon.

2. Heat an extra-large nonstick oven-going skillet over medium heat. Add salmon, herb side down. Cook for 3 minutes or until golden brown. Turn salmon; pour herbed lemon juice over salmon. Place pan in oven and bake for 7 minutes or until salmon flakes easily when tested with a fork.

3. Transfer salmon to serving plates; drizzle with pan juices. Top with additional shredded lemon peel and snipped fresh herbs.

FOR 8 SERVINGS Prepare using method above, except in Step 1 cut salmon into eight equal pieces and shred 2 teaspoons peel from lemons. Cut lemons in half; juice half the lemons.

PER SERVING *294 cal., 21 g fat (7 g sat. fat), 78 mg chol., 401 mg sodium, 3 g carb., 1 g fiber, 24 g pro.*

PREP **15 minutes**
BAKE **7 minutes at 350°F**

4 servings	ingredients	8 servings
1 lb.	skinless salmon fillet	2 lb.
1	lemon	2
1 Tbsp.	snipped fresh dill	2 Tbsp.
1 Tbsp.	snipped fresh tarragon or lemon thyme	2 Tbsp.
1 Tbsp.	snipped fresh parsley or bias-sliced chives	2 Tbsp.
½ tsp.	salt	1 tsp.
½ tsp.	black pepper	1 tsp.
2 Tbsp.	butter, softened	4 Tbsp.
	Lemon peel and fresh herbs (optional)	

Citrus Salmon with Broccoli

To be sure the salmon releases from the skillet and doesn't stick when it's time to turn it, let it cook until the bottom is golden. When the fish has a crust, it will easily release from the pan.

1. Slice half the lemon into thin slices; set aside. Juice remaining lemon into a 1 cup measure; add water to equal ½ cup. Stir in sugar. Set aside.

2. In an extra-large nonstick skillet heat butter over medium-high heat. Sprinkle salmon with salt and pepper; add to skillet. Cook for 2 to 3 minutes or until bottom is golden; turn fillets. Add lemon juice mixture. Top with snipped dill and lemon slices. Reduce heat to medium; cover and cook 5 to 6 minutes more or until fish flakes easily when tested with a fork.

3. Meanwhile, in another skillet heat oil over medium heat. Quarter broccoli lengthwise into long spears; add to skillet along with garlic. Cook broccoli and garlic in hot oil over medium heat for 8 to 10 minutes or until crisp-tender, turning often. Serve salmon with broccoli; pour pan juices over salmon. If desired, serve with additional lemon slices and fresh dill.

FOR 8 SERVINGS Prepare using method above, except in Step 1 slice one of the lemons into thin slices. Juice remaining lemon into a 2-cup measure; add water to equal 1 cup.

PER SERVING *363 cal., 25 g fat (8 g sat. fat), 78 mg chol., 277 mg sodium, 12 g carb., 3 g fiber, 26 g pro.*

START TO FINISH **22 minutes**

4 servings	ingredients	8 servings
1	lemon	2
1 Tbsp.	sugar	2 Tbsp.
2 Tbsp.	butter	4 Tbsp.
4	4-oz. skinless salmon fillets	8
	Salt	
	Black pepper	
1 Tbsp.	snipped fresh dill	2 Tbsp.
1 Tbsp.	olive oil	2 Tbsp.
1 lb.	broccoli, trimmed	2 lb.
4	cloves garlic, peeled and sliced	8
	Lemon slices and fresh dill (optional)	

Stir-Fry Shrimp with Cheesy Grits

A Southern classic is given a Mexican spin in this dish that incorporates sweet peppers, Mexican cheese, chili powder, and a simple cilantro drizzle on top.

START TO FINISH 25 minutes

4 servings	ingredients	8 servings
2	red and/or yellow sweet peppers	4
½ cup	quick-cooking hominy grits	1 cup
½ cup (2 oz.)	shredded Mexican cheese blend	1 cup (4 oz.)
	Salt and black pepper	
1½ lb.	medium shrimp, peeled and deveined, tails intact	3 lb.
½ tsp.	chili powder	1 tsp.
¼ cup	olive oil	½ cup
1 cup	cilantro sprigs	2 cups
1 Tbsp.	cider vinegar	2 Tbsp.

1. Halve, seed, and coarsely chop peppers. In a medium saucepan heat 1¾ cups water to boiling. Stir in grits and peppers. Return to boiling. Reduce heat. Simmer, covered, 5 minutes, until most of the water is absorbed and grits are tender. Stir in cheese. Sprinkle with salt and pepper. Cover; keep warm.

2. In a bowl toss shrimp with chili powder. Heat 1 tablespoon oil in large skillet over medium-high heat. Add shrimp. Cook and stir 3 to 4 minutes or until shrimp are opaque.

3. In a food processor combine remaining oil, cilantro, vinegar, and 2 tablespoons water. Drizzle processed mixture over shrimp and grits. Serve with lemon and cilantro.

FOR 8 SERVINGS Prepare using method above, except in Step 1 heat 3½ cups water. In Step 2 heat 2 tablespoons oil in an extra-large skillet. In Step 3 use ¼ cup water.

PER SERVING *385 cal., 21 g fat (5 g sat. fat), 185 mg chol., 423 mg sodium, 21 g carb., 3 g fiber, 29 g pro.*

Coconut Shrimp with Mango Sauce

Shrimp are sold by size and are assigned a set of numbers that indicates how many shrimp per pound. For instance, shrimp labeled 31/35 would be considered large—and there are between 31 and 35 shrimp per pound.

PREP 30 minutes
BAKE 8 minutes at 425°F

4 servings	ingredients	8 servings
12 oz.	fresh or frozen large shrimp in shells	24 oz.
2	medium mangoes, seeded, peeled, and chopped	4
¼ cup	honey	½ cup
1 tsp.	finely shredded lime peel	2 tsp.
2 Tbsp.	lime juice	¼ cup
⅛ tsp.	cayenne pepper	¼ tsp.
1 Tbsp.	snipped fresh cilantro	2 Tbsp.
	Nonstick cooking spray	
	Salt	
1 cup	unsweetened flaked coconut	2 cups
	Fresh cilantro sprigs (optional)	
	Lime wedges	

1. Thaw shrimp, if frozen. Preheat oven to 425°F. For sauce, in a blender combine 1 cup of the mango, the honey, lime juice, and cayenne pepper. Cover and blend until smooth. Remove ¼ cup of the sauce and pour into a shallow dish. Transfer the remaining sauce to a serving bowl for dipping. Sprinkle with lime peel and snipped cilantro.

2. Line a baking sheet with foil; lightly coat foil with cooking spray; set aside. Peel and devein shrimp, leaving tails intact if desired. Rinse shrimp; pat dry with paper towels. Sprinkle with salt. Place coconut in a shallow dish. Dip shrimp into reserved mango sauce, then into coconut, turning and pressing shrimp to coat. Place on prepared baking sheet. Bake, uncovered, for 8 to 10 minutes or until shrimp are opaque and coconut is golden.

3. Garnish shrimp with the remaining chopped mango and, if desired, additional cilantro. Serve with dipping sauce and lime wedges.

FOR 8 SERVINGS Prepare using method above, except in Step 1 use 2 cups of mango. Remove ½ cup of the mango sauce and pour into a shallow dish.

PER SERVING *414 cal., 20 g fat (17 g sat. fat), 129 mg chol., 285 mg sodium, 44 g carb., 7 g fiber, 20 g pro.*

Shrimp Kabobs with Lemon Marinade

Be sure not to marinate the shrimp any longer than 15 minutes; the acid in the marinade will start to "cook" and toughen the shrimp.

1. Thaw shrimp, if frozen. Peel and devein shrimp, leaving tails intact if desired. Rinse shrimp; pat dry with paper towels.

2. For marinade, in a large bowl combine olive oil, lemon peel, lemon juice, and parsley. Set aside half the marinade. Toss shrimp with the remaining oil marinade. Cover and marinate in the refrigerator for 15 minutes.

3. Drain shrimp, discarding marinade. Thread shrimp onto eight 8-inch skewers (see tip, page 75).

4. For a charcoal or gas grill, place kabobs on the grill rack directly over medium heat. Cover and grill for 4 to 6 minutes or until shrimp are opaque, turning once halfway through grilling.

5. Transfer shrimp to a serving dish. Drizzle with the reserved marinade. Serve with cherry tomatoes and green onions.

PER SERVING *271 cal., 12 g fat (2 g sat. fat), 259 mg chol., 255 mg sodium, 4 g carb., 1 g fiber, 35 g pro.*

PREP **25 minutes**
MARINATE **15 minutes**
GRILL **4 minutes**

4 servings	ingredients	8 servings
1½ lb.	fresh or frozen jumbo shrimp in shells	3 lb.
⅓ cup	olive oil	⅔ cup
2 tsp.	finely shredded lemon peel	4 tsp.
¼ cup	lemon juice	½ cup
1 Tbsp.	snipped fresh parsley	2 Tbsp.
8	cherry tomatoes, quartered	16
2	green onions, sliced	4

Grilled Shrimp and Pineapple Kabobs

On a warm summer night when you have just minutes to make dinner, toss these shrimp kabobs on the barbie—they're very fast (just under 30 minutes start to finish) and tasty.

1. Peel and devein shrimp; thread onto four skewers (see tip, page 75). In a small saucepan combine 4 tablespoons of the marmalade, the water, and soy sauce. Brush some of the marmalade-soy sauce mixture onto shrimp and pineapple.

2. For a charcoal or gas grill, place kabobs and pineapple on the grill rack directly over medium heat. Cover and grill for 8 to 10 minutes or until shrimp are opaque and pineapple is heated through, turning once halfway through grilling. Remove from heat; cover to keep warm.

3. Meanwhile, heat rice according to package directions. Transfer rice to a serving bowl; stir in the remaining marmalade and the cilantro.

4. In a saucepan heat remaining marmalade-soy sauce to boiling. Serve kabobs and pineapple with rice and marmalade-soy sauce.

PER SERVING *322 cal., 3 g fat (0 g sat. fat), 172 mg chol., 451 mg sodium, 49 g carb., 2 g fiber, 25 g pro.*

PREP 20 minutes   GRILL 8 minutes

4 servings	ingredients	8 servings
1 lb.	uncooked jumbo shrimp	2 lb.
4	½-inch slices fresh pineapple	8
6 Tbsp.	orange marmalade	¾ cup
½ cup	water	1 cup
1 Tbsp.	soy sauce	2 Tbsp.
1	8.8-oz. pouch cooked long grain rice	2
¼ cup	snipped fresh cilantro	½ cup

CHAPTER 5

Sides

Keep the entrée simple—a piece of grilled or roasted meat, poultry, or fish—and round out the menu with a special salad or side dish.

138

144

153

Spiced Nuts and Zucchini Corn Bread

Finely chopped salt-and-pepper mixed nuts are the surprise ingredient in this cheesy corn bread made moist with shredded zucchini and applesauce.

1. Preheat oven to 300°F. Grease an 8×8×2-inch baking pan; set aside. In a large bowl stir together flour, cornmeal, nuts, sugar, baking powder, and salt; set aside.

2. In a bowl whisk together the eggs, butter, and applesauce. Stir in the corn, zucchini, cheese, and onion. Add egg mixture all at once to cornmeal mixture. Stir just until moistened. Pour batter into prepared pan.

3. Bake 50 to 60 minutes, just until edges are golden brown. Cool slightly; serve warm.

FOR 18 SERVINGS Prepare using method above, except in Step 1 use a 13×9×2-inch baking pan.

PER SERVING *201 cal., 11 g fat (5 g sat. fat), 67 mg chol., 326 mg sodium, 21 g carb., 1 g fiber, 5 g pro.*

PREP 25 minutes
BAKE 50 minutes at 300°F

9 servings	ingredients	18 servings
½ cup	all-purpose flour	1 cup
½ cup	yellow cornmeal	1 cup
¼ cup	spiced mixed nuts (salt and pepper mixed nuts), finely chopped	½ cup
3 Tbsp.	sugar	⅓ cup
2 tsp.	baking powder	4 tsp.
⅛ tsp.	salt	¼ tsp.
2	eggs	4
¼ cup	butter, melted	½ cup
¼ cup	unsweetened applesauce	½ cup
½	14.75-oz. can cream-style corn	1
½ cup	coarsely shredded zucchini	1 cup
½ cup (2 oz.)	shredded sharp cheddar cheese	1 cup (4 oz.)
¼ cup	finely chopped onion	½ cup

Corn Bread Stuffing with Sausage

Buy corn bread muffins from the bakery section of your supermarket or make a quick batch from a boxed mix.

1. Preheat oven to 325°F. Spread muffin pieces in a 15×10×1-inch baking pan. Lightly toast in oven, uncovered, for 10 minutes, stirring once. Cool on a wire rack.

2. In a large skillet cook sausage until brown. Drain fat, reserving 1 tablespoon drippings in skillet. Set sausage aside. In the same skillet cook onion in reserved drippings for 3 to 5 minutes or until onion starts to brown. Stir in spinach, fennel, salt, and pepper.

3. In a large bowl combine muffin pieces, sausage, and spinach mixture. Drizzle with broth to moisten, tossing lightly to combine. Spoon into a 2-quart baking dish.

4. Bake, uncovered, about 45 minutes or until top is browned and stuffing is heated through.

FOR 8 SERVINGS Prepare using method above, except in Step 1 use two 15×10×1-inch baking pans; rotate pans halfway through toasting time. In Step 2 reserve 2 tablespoons drippings. In Step 3 use a 4-quart baking dish.

PER SERVING *166 cal., 9 g fat (3 g sat. fat), 26 mg chol., 499 mg sodium, 16 g carb., 1 g fiber, 5 g pro.*

PREP 25 minutes
BAKE 45 minutes at 325°F

11 servings	ingredients	22 servings
8 (4 cups)	corn bread muffins, broken into large pieces	16 (8 cups)
8 oz.	bulk pork sausage	1 lb.
1	medium onion, cut into wedges	2
4 cups	fresh spinach	8 cups
1 tsp.	fennel seeds, crushed	2 tsp.
½ tsp.	salt	1 tsp.
¼ tsp.	black pepper	½ tsp.
1 to 1⅓ cups	turkey or chicken broth	2 to 2⅔ cups

Curried Butternut Squash Soup

For a little something different, try this creamy curried soup as a starter for a Thanksgiving feast.

1. In a very large saucepan cook onion in hot butter over medium heat about 10 minutes or until tender and translucent. Stir in curry powder, ginger, and salt. Cook 30 seconds more.

2. Stir in chicken broth and water; bring to boiling. Add squash. Return to boiling; reduce heat. Simmer, covered, about 40 minutes or until squash is tender.

3. Cool soup slightly. Transfer half the soup at a time to a blender or food processor. Blend or process until smooth. Return all soup to saucepan. Stir in coconut milk, half-and-half, and chopped cilantro. Heat through. Sprinkle with fresh cilantro.

FOR 12 SERVINGS Prepare using method above, except in Step 1 use an 8-quart Dutch oven.

PER SERVING *285 cal., 24 g fat (19 g sat. fat), 23 mg chol., 418 mg sodium, 18 g carb., 4 g fiber, 4 g pro.*

PREP 25 minutes
COOK 40 minutes

6 servings	ingredients	12 servings
½ cup	chopped onion	1 cup
3 Tbsp.	butter	6 Tbsp.
2 tsp.	red curry powder or curry powder	4 tsp.
2 tsp.	grated fresh ginger	4 tsp.
½ tsp.	salt	1 tsp.
1	14-oz. can reduced-sodium chicken broth	2
1¼ cups	water	2½ cups
1½ lb. (4 cups)	butternut squash, peeled, seeded, and cut into 1-inch cubes	3 lb. (8 cups)
1	14-oz. can unsweetened coconut milk	2
½ cup	half-and-half or light cream	1 cup
⅓ cup	chopped fresh cilantro	⅔ cup
	Fresh cilantro (optional)	

Citrusy Mashed Squash with Toasted Pecans

This rich squash puree infused with maple, orange, and sage is perfect with roast turkey, roast pork loin, or ham.

1. In a 5- or 6-quart Dutch oven cook squash in lightly salted boiling water, covered, for 15 minutes or until tender when pierced with a fork. Drain.

2. Meanwhile, in a heavy skillet melt the butter over medium heat, whisking frequently until golden brown, 5 to 6 minutes. Transfer half the cooked squash to a food processor. Add butter, sour cream, maple syrup, orange and lemon peels, salt, and pepper. Cover and process until smooth. Place remaining squash in a bowl; add pureed mixture. Mash slightly. Stir in fresh sage.

3. Top with pecans, green onions and/or sage leaves, and additional citrus peel.

FOR 12 SERVINGS Prepare using method above, except in Step 1 use an 8-quart Dutch oven. In Step 2 transfer one-fourth of the cooked squash with half the butter, sour cream, maple syrup, orange and lemon peels, salt, and pepper. Repeat to puree a second one-fourth squash.

PER SERVING *176 cal., 9 g fat (3 g sat. fat), 12 mg chol., 258 mg sodium, 25 g carb., 4 g fiber, 2 g pro.*

PREP **15 minutes**
COOK **20 minutes**

6 servings	ingredients	12 servings
3 lb.	butternut squash, peeled, seeded, and cut into chunks	6 lb.
2 Tbsp.	butter	4 Tbsp.
⅓ cup	sour cream	⅔ cup
¼ cup	maple syrup	½ cup
2 tsp.	finely shredded orange peel	4 tsp.
2 tsp.	finely shredded lemon peel	4 tsp.
¾ tsp.	salt	1½ tsp.
¼ tsp.	black pepper	½ tsp.
2 Tbsp.	snipped fresh sage	4 Tbsp.
½ cup	pecan halves, toasted and coarsely chopped (see tip, page 28)	1 cup
	Sliced green onions and/or fresh sage leaves and finely shredded orange and lemon peels	

Sweet Potatoes with Pecans and Blue Cheese

The sweetness of the oven-roasted potatoes is beautifully balanced by the salty tang of the blue cheese in this easy but elegant side. The pecans add a pleasing richness and crunch.

PREP 30 minutes
BAKE 30 minutes at 375°F

6 servings	ingredients	12 servings
2 (1½ pounds)	large sweet potatoes, peeled and cut lengthwise into narrow wedges	4 (3 pounds)
1	small sweet onion, cut into 1-inch pieces	2
4 Tbsp.	olive oil	½ cup
1 tsp.	salt	2 tsp.
½ tsp.	black pepper	1 tsp.
1 Tbsp.	butter	2 Tbsp.
⅓ cup	broken pecans	⅔ cup
1 Tbsp.	packed light brown sugar	2 Tbsp.
4 tsp.	cider vinegar	3 Tbsp.
1½ tsp.	honey	3 tsp.
1	clove garlic, minced	2
2 Tbsp.	crumbled blue cheese or finely shredded white cheddar cheese	¼ cup

1. Preheat oven to 375°F. In a 15×10×1-inch baking pan combine sweet potatoes and onion. Drizzle with half the oil; sprinkle with half the salt and pepper. Toss gently to combine. Spread in a single layer. Bake for 30 to 35 minutes or until potatoes are tender, stirring once.

2. Meanwhile, in a small skillet melt butter over medium heat. Stir in pecans, brown sugar, and ¼ teaspoon salt. Cook and stir for 2 to 3 minutes or until pecans are coated in the brown sugar mixture. Spread pecans on a sheet of foil; cool completely.

3. For dressing, in a small bowl whisk together vinegar, honey, garlic, the remaining salt, and the remaining pepper. Slowly whisk in the remaining oil until combined. Whisk in half the cheese.

4. To serve, transfer sweet potatoes and onion to a serving platter. Drizzle with dressing. Sprinkle with pecans and the remaining cheese.

FOR 12 SERVINGS Prepare using method above, except in Step 1 use two 15×10×1-inch baking pans. In Step 2 use ½ teaspoon salt.

PER SERVING *241 cal., 16 g fat (3 g sat. fat), 7 mg chol., 487 mg sodium, 23 g carb., 3 g fiber, 3 g pro.*

Three-Potato Salad with Mustard Dressing

Vinaigrette-dressed potato salads are much lighter than mayo-dressed versions. This one can be served warm or at room temperature and goes great with grilled steak.

1. In a medium skillet heat the ½ teaspoon oil over medium heat. Add onion; cook and stir until tender. Set aside.

2. For salad dressing, in a small bowl combine vinegar and sugar, stirring to dissolve. Whisk in mustard. Add the 4 teaspoons oil in a thin, steady stream, whisking to combine; set aside.

3. In a covered large saucepan combine potatoes and enough cold water to cover. Stir in salt; bring to boiling. Boil potatoes 8 to 10 minutes or until tender.

4. Drain potatoes; transfer to a large bowl. Toss warm potatoes with cooked onion, spinach, and olives. Cover bowl and let stand to wilt spinach. After 2 minutes, add salad dressing and toss to coat. Serve warm or at room temperature.

FOR 12 SERVINGS Prepare using method above, except in Step 1 use 1 teaspoon oil. In Step 2 use 3 tablespoons oil. In Step 3 cook potatoes in 5- to 6-quart Dutch oven.

PER SERVING 145 cal., 5 g fat (1 g sat. fat), 0 g chol., 362 mg sodium, 23 g carb., 3 g fiber, 3 g pro.

PREP 20 minutes
COOK 18 minutes
STAND 2 minutes

6 servings	ingredients	12 servings
½ tsp.	olive oil	1 tsp.
¼ cup	chopped red onion	½ cup
3 Tbsp.	white balsamic vinegar	⅓ cup
¾ tsp.	sugar	1½ tsp.
4 tsp.	whole-grain mustard	3 Tbsp.
4 tsp.	olive oil	3 Tbsp.
1½ lb.	assorted baby potatoes, such as red, yellow, fingerling, and purple, quartered	3 lb.
½ tsp.	salt	1 tsp.
1 cup	baby spinach or torn radicchio	2 cups
¼ cup	chopped pitted Kalamata olives	½ cup

Blue Cheese-Garlic Potatoes

Flavored with blue cheese and thin slices of caramelized garlic, these potatoes would be at home on the menu of a pricey steakhouse—but they couldn't be simpler to make. Add crushed red pepper to your taste—mild, hot, or hotter.

1. In a Dutch oven combine potatoes, water to cover, and about half the salt. Bring to boiling. Reduce heat and simmer, covered, until potatoes are tender. Reserving ¼ cup cooking water, drain potatoes and return to pot.

2. In a skillet cook garlic in hot olive oil for 1 minute until garlic starts to brown. Mash into potatoes with reserved cooking water, crumbled blue cheese, remaining salt, and crushed red pepper to taste.

FOR 12 SERVINGS Prepare using method above, except in Step 1 cook potatoes in a large Dutch oven. Reserve ½ cup cooking water.

PER SERVING *156 cal., 9 g fat (3 g sat. fat), 8 mg chol., 453 mg sodium, 15 g carb., 1 g fiber, 4 g pro.*

PREP 20 minutes
COOK 12 minutes

6 servings	ingredients	12 servings
1½ lb.	russet or Yukon gold potatoes, peeled and cubed	3 lb.
¾ tsp.	salt	1½ tsp.
2 Tbsp.	olive oil	¼ cup
1	clove garlic, thinly sliced	2
2 oz.	crumbled blue cheese	4 oz.
	Crushed red pepper flakes	

Parmesan-Roasted Cauliflower

The high heat of the oven works magic on mild-mannered cauliflower. It gets crispy and delightfully browned on the tips of the florets—and tender and toothsome everywhere else.

1. Preheat oven to 425°F. Place cauliflower in a 15×10×1-inch baking pan and toss with olive oil, salt, and pepper. Roast for 20 minutes. Sprinkle with Parmesan cheese and toss to combine. Roast 5 minutes.

2. Meanwhile, in a medium skillet, melt butter. Add garlic; cook 20 seconds. Add almonds and panko and stir to coat with butter. Cook over medium-low to medium heat until golden. Transfer cauliflower to a serving dish and top with the almond-panko mixture.

FOR 16 SERVINGS Prepare using method above, except in Step 1 use two 15×10×1-inch baking pans, rotating pans once halfway through baking time.

PER SERVING *175 cal., 14 g fat (5 g sat. fat), 19 mg chol., 319 mg sodium, 9 g carb., 3 g fiber, 6 g pro.*

PREP **15 minutes**
ROAST **25 minutes at 425°F**
COOK **12 minutes**

8 servings	ingredients	16 servings
6 cups	cauliflower florets	12 cups
1 Tbsp.	olive oil	2 Tbsp.
	Salt	
	Black pepper	
½ cup	freshly shredded Parmesan cheese	1 cup
¼ cup	butter	½ cup
2	cloves garlic, chopped	4
⅔ cup	slivered almonds, chopped	1⅓ cup
⅔ cup	panko or coarse bread crumbs	1⅓ cup

Seared Brussels Sprouts

Crisp-fried shallot rings crown these skillet-browned Brussels sprouts.

PREP 25 minutes
COOK 10 minutes

4 servings	ingredients	8 servings
1	shallot thinly sliced and separated into rings	2
1 Tbsp.	all-purpose flour	2 Tbsp.
	Canola oil	
	Salt	
1 Tbsp.	olive oil	2 Tbsp.
12 oz. (3 cups)	fresh Brussels sprouts, trimmed and halved	1½ lb. (6 cups)
¼ cup	white wine	½ cup

1. Place flour in a small bowl. Toss shallot rings in flour then let stand 10 to 15 minutes to become sticky.* In an extra-large skillet heat 1 inch of oil over medium-high heat. Using a slotted spoon, add half the shallots. Fry 3 to 4 minutes, until crisp and dark golden brown. Remove from oil; drain on a double thickness of paper towels. Fry remaining shallots. Sprinkle with salt; set aside. Discard oil; wipe skillet clean.

2. Add half the olive oil to the skillet and return to medium heat. Carefully arrange half the sprouts, cut sides down, in the hot skillet. Cook, uncovered, 3 to 4 minutes or until sprouts are well browned. Remove sprouts from pan. Repeat with remaining oil and sprouts. Return reserved sprouts to the skillet. Add wine; deglaze pan by scraping up any browned bits from the bottom. Cover and cook 4 to 6 minutes more or until tender. Season to taste with salt and pepper. Transfer to a serving dish and top with the crispy shallots.

*TIP Crispy shallots may be prepared up to 4 hours ahead and stored in a tightly covered container.

PER SERVING *144 cal., 10 g fat (1 g sat. fat), 0 g chol., 59 mg sodium, 10 g carb., 3 g fiber, 3 g pro.*

Roasted Vegetables and Chickpeas

Carrots, sweet potatoes, white potatoes, and red onion mingle with chickpeas in this hearty vegetable side. Try it with beef roast—or serve it on its own with whole grain bread or rolls as a vegetarian main dish.

1. Position an oven rack in center of oven. Preheat oven to 425°F. Place all vegetables, garlic, and chickpeas in a large shallow roasting pan. In a small bowl combine the oil, rosemary, brown sugar, salt, and pepper. Drizzle over vegetables; toss well to coat.

2. Roast, uncovered, about 45 minutes or until vegetables are lightly browned and tender, stirring twice.

FOR 16 SERVINGS Prepare using method above, except in Step 1 position two oven racks toward center of oven, allowing enough room for pans and air circulation. Use two large shallow roasting pans, rotating plans once halfway through roasting.

PER SERVING *223 cal., 4 g fat (0 g sat. fat), 0 g chol., 301 mg sodium, 42 g carb., 7 g fiber, 6 g pro.*

PREP **30 minutes**
ROAST **45 minutes at 425°F**

8 servings	ingredients	16 servings
1 lb.	carrots, peeled and cut into 2-inch pieces	2 lb.
1 lb.	sweet potatoes, peeled and cut into chunks	2 lb.
1	large red onion, peeled, , halved, and cut into 1-inch wedges	2
1 lb.	red or russet potatoes, cut into cubes	2 lb.
6	cloves garlic, minced	12
1	16-oz. can chickpeas (garbanzos), rinsed and drained	2
2 to 3 Tbsp.	vegetable oil or olive oil	4 to 6 Tbsp.
1 tsp.	dried rosemary, crushed	2 tsp.
1 tsp.	packed brown sugar or granulated sugar	2 tsp.
½ tsp.	kosher salt	1 tsp.
½ tsp.	freshly ground black pepper	1 tsp.

Roasted Asparagus-Orange Salad

Asparagus is the sweetest and most tender in mid- to late-spring. This warm-to-room-temperature salad is the perfect accompaniment to roast chicken.

1. Preheat oven to 400°F. Place asparagus in a 15×10×1-inch baking pan. Drizzle with oil, sprinkle with salt, and toss to coat. Roast, uncovered, for 15 to 20 minutes, until asparagus is crisp-tender, tossing once. Transfer to a serving platter.

2. Meanwhile, for dressing, remove enough zest from half the orange to equal ¼ teaspoon, then juice the half to equal about 4 teaspoons. Peel and slice the remaining half. For dressing, in a screw-top jar combine orange peel, orange juice, garlic, mustard, fennel seeds, olive oil, and vinegar. Cover and shake well.

3. Drizzle a little of the dressing on the asparagus; toss to coat. Carefully toss orange slices and asparagus together. Pass remaining dressing.

FOR 8 SERVINGS Prepare using method above, except in Step 2 zest one orange to equal ½ teaspoon. Juice half an orange to equal about 3 tablespoons. Peel and slice remaining half and whole orange.

PER SERVING *85 cal., 5 g fat (1 g sat. fat), 0 g chol., 90 mg sodium, 8 g carb., 3 g fiber, 3 g pro.*

PREP **10 minutes**
ROAST **15 minutes**

4 servings	ingredients	8 servings
1 lb.	green, white, and/or purple asparagus spears, trimmed	2 lb.
1½ tsp.	olive oil	1 Tbsp.
⅛ tsp.	salt	¼ tsp.
1	orange	2
½ clove	garlic, minced	1 clove
½ tsp.	Dijon mustard	1 tsp.
¼ tsp.	fennel seeds, crushed	½ tsp.
1 Tbsp.	olive oil	2 Tbsp.
1½ tsp.	cider vinegar	1 Tbsp.

Basil-Tomato Salad

A baguette is turned into crispy croutonlike breadsticks to accompany this flavorful salad of lettuce, tomatoes, toasted pine nuts, Parmesan cheese—and a surprising amount of basil.

1. For lemon vinaigrette, in a small screw-top jar combine the ½ cup olive oil, lemon peel, lemon juice, garlic, sugar, salt, and pepper. Cover and shake well.

2. Preheat oven to 425°F. Split baguette in half horizontally. In a small bowl combine 2 tablespoons olive oil and garlic. Brush onto cut sides of bread. Cut each half lengthwise into 3 or 4 breadsticks. Place on baking sheet. Bake 3 to 5 minutes or until toasted. Transfer to wire rack; cool.

3. In a large bowl combine lettuce and basil. Layer tomatoes, pine nuts, and cheese on top. Serve with breadsticks and lemon vinaigrette.

FOR 12 SERVINGS Prepare using method above, except in Step 1 use 1 cup olive oil. In Step 2 use ¼ cup oil.

PER SERVING *449 cal., 33 g fat (6 g sat. fat), 8 mg chol., 502 mg sodium, 30 g carb., 3 g fiber, 13 g pro.*

PREP **25 minutes**
BAKE **3 minutes at 350°F**

6 servings	ingredients	12 servings
½ cup	olive oil	1 cup
1 tsp.	finely shredded lemon peel	2 tsp.
⅓ cup	lemon juice	⅔ cup
4	cloves garlic, minced	8
1 tsp.	sugar	2 tsp.
¼ tsp.	salt	½ tsp.
¼ tsp.	black pepper	½ tsp.
1	small baguette or French roll	2
2 Tbsp.	olive oil	¼ cup
2	cloves garlic, minced	4
1 (6 cups)	small head green leaf lettuce, torn	2 (12 cups)
3 cups	fresh basil, torn	6 cups
2 cups	grape tomatoes, halved, or chopped plum tomatoes	4 cups
½ cup	pine nuts, toasted (see tip, page 28)	1 cup
2 oz.	Parmesan cheese, shaved	4 oz.

Tiny-Tomato Salad with Cucumbers and Sherry-Ginger Vinaigrette

English cucumbers are longer and more slender than standard cucumbers. They are most often sold wrapped in plastic. To score the cucumber, drag a fork down it from top to bottom, repeating until the entire cucumber is marked.

PREP 30 minutes
CHILL 1 hour

10 servings	ingredients	20 servings
1½ cups	yellow pear tomatoes, halved	3 cups
1½ cups	orange cherry tomatoes, halved	3 cups
1½ cups	red grape tomatoes, halved	3 cups
1	English cucumber, scored and cut into ¼-inch rounds	2
2 Tbsp.	sliced green onion	¼ cup
⅓ cup	vegetable oil	⅔ cup
1 Tbsp.	sherry vinegar or white wine vinegar	2 Tbsp.
1 Tbsp.	grated fresh ginger	2 Tbsp.
1 tsp.	sugar	2 tsp.
½ tsp.	salt	1 tsp.
½ tsp.	cracked black pepper	1 tsp.

1. In a large bowl combine yellow tomatoes, orange tomatoes, grape tomatoes, cucumber, and green onion. Toss gently to combine.

2. For vinaigrette, in a screw-top jar combine oil, vinegar, ginger, sugar, salt, and pepper. Cover and shake well. Pour over tomato salad; toss to coat. Cover and chill salad for 1 to 4 hours. Stir gently before serving.

PER SERVING *83 cal., 7 g fat (1 g sat. fat), 0 mg chol., 133 mg sodium, 4 g carb., 1 g fiber, 1 g pro.*

Mandarin Cream Salad with Coconut-Crumb Crust

This retro-style gelatin salad could be dessert. A shortbread-coconut crust is layered with sweetened cream cheese and glistening orange gelatin studded with mandarin oranges. Take it to a potluck and you will bring none of it home.

1. Preheat oven to 375°F. For crust, in a medium bowl stir together crushed cookies, coconut, melted butter, and orange peel until combined. Pat evenly into the bottom of a 2-quart baking dish. Bake for 12 to 14 minutes or until crust is light brown. Cool completely on a wire rack.

2. For topping, in a medium bowl stir together gelatin and boiling water until gelatin is dissolved. Cool completely at room temperature.

3. Meanwhile, for filling, in a large mixing bowl beat cream cheese and sugar with an electric mixer on medium for 1 to 2 minutes or until light and fluffy. Fold in whipped topping. Evenly spread cream cheese mixture over cooled crust. Chill at least 30 minutes.

4. Stir orange sections into gelatin topping. Carefully pour topping over chilled cream cheese filling. Cover and chill about 3 hours or until firm. Salad may be chilled up to 24 hours. To serve, cut into squares.

FOR 18 SERVINGS Prepare using method above, except in Step 1 use a 3-quart baking dish.

PER SERVING *296 cal., 16 g fat (10 g sat. fat), 30 mg chol., 191 mg sodium, 34 g carb., 1 g fiber, 3 g pro.*

PREP **30 minutes**
BAKE **12 minutes at 375°F**
COOL **1 hour**
CHILL **3 hours 30 minutes**

9 servings	ingredients	18 servings
1 cup (18 cookies)	finely crushed shortbread cookies	2 cups (36 cookies)
⅓ cup	flaked coconut	⅔ cup
¼ cup	butter, melted	½ cup
½ tsp.	finely shredded orange peel	1 tsp.
1	3-oz. pkg. orange-flavor gelatin	2
1 cup	boiling water	2 cups
½	8-oz. pkg. cream cheese, softened	1
⅓ cup	sugar	¾ cup
½	8-oz. container frozen whipped dessert topping, thawed	1
1	11-oz. can mandarin orange sections, drained	2

Beet, Blue Cheese, and Almond Salad

Marcona almonds are a variety that comes from Spain. They have a higher fat content and sweeter, richer flavor than California-grown almonds. Look for them at whole-foods stores and wine shops. They can be found both raw and fried in sunflower or olive oil and salted. If you can't find them, substitute regular almonds.

PREP 25 minutes
COOK 20 minutes
COOL 1 hour

6 servings	ingredients	12 servings
7 (2½ lb.)	medium beets	14 (5 lb.)
1	small clove garlic	2
	Kosher salt	
3 Tbsp.	extra virgin olive oil	6 Tbsp.
2 Tbsp.	lemon juice	¼ cup
1 tsp.	salt	2 tsp.
¾ tsp.	black pepper	1½ tsp.
8 oz.	creamy blue cheese	1 lb.
2 oz.	Marcona almonds, toasted (see tip, page 28)	4 oz.
1 Tbsp.	chopped fresh parsley	2 Tbsp.

1. Trim and peel the beets. Cut six beets into bite-size pieces. Place in a steamer rack over a pan of boiling water. Cover the pan and steam for 20 minutes or until tender.

2. Coarsely grate remaining beet; place in a large bowl. For dressing, mash the garlic with a pinch of salt to make a paste; add to grated beet along with the oil, lemon juice, 1 teaspoon salt, and pepper. When beets are cooked, toss them with the dressing. Cool to room temperature.

3. Crumble blue cheese over individual salads and sprinkle with almonds and parsley.

FOR 12 SERVINGS Prepare using method above, except in Step 1 cut 12 beets into bite-size pieces. In Step 2 grate remaining beets and use 2 teaspoons salt.

PER SERVING *333 cal., 23 g fat (8 g sat. fat), 28 mg chol., 1,005 mg sodium, 21 g carb., 6 g fiber, 13 g pro.*

Penne Salad with Asparagus, Copocollo, and Three Cheeses

The asparagus in this pasta salad is essentially blanched—cooked for just 2 minutes and then doused with cold water to preserve the tender crunch and bright green color.

1. In a large pot cook pasta according to package directions until tender but firm to the bite. Add asparagus to pot the last 2 minutes of cooking. Drain pasta and asparagus. Rinse well in cold water; drain again. Transfer pasta and asparagus to an extra-large bowl.

2. Add olives, red pepper, copocollo, cubed cheeses, and basil to pasta mixture. Toss gently to combine. Cover and chill for 2 to 24 hours before serving.

PER SERVING *263 cal., 15 g fat (5 g sat. fat), 22 mg chol., 581 mg sodium, 20 g carb., 1 g fiber, 10 g pro.*

PREP **30 minutes**
CHILL **2 hours**

10 servings	ingredients	20 servings
8 oz.	dried penne pasta	16 oz.
8 oz.	asparagus, trimmed and cut into 1½-inch lengths	1 lb.
½ cup	halved pitted Kalamata olives	1 cup
½ cup	chopped red sweet pepper	1 cup
3 oz.	copocollo or prosciutto, thinly sliced and coarsely chopped	6 oz.
3 oz.	Fontina cheese, cut into cubes	6 oz.
2 oz.	sharp cheddar cheese, cut into cubes	4 oz.
2 oz.	Gouda cheese, cut into cubes	4 oz.
¼ cup	coarsely chopped fresh basil	½ cup
¾ cup	creamy garlic dressing or creamy Italian dressing	1½ cups

BLT Salad with Buttermilk Dressing

Romaine lettuce heads can be quite large. Look for heads that are on the smaller side for this recipe. Each person gets a half of a head—grilled and topped with tomatoes, bacon, and buttermilk dressing—as a side dish.

1. For salad dressing, in a small bowl whisk together crème fraîche, mayonnaise, dill, vinegar, and garlic. Whisk in buttermilk. Season to taste with salt and pepper.

2. Preheat oven to 375°F. Arrange bacon on a baking sheet; bake about 15 minutes or until crispy. Transfer bacon to paper towels. Crumble bacon; set aside.

3. Cut each head of lettuce in half lengthwise. Brush lettuce halves all over with oil; season with salt and pepper. For a charcoal or gas grill, place lettuce on the grill rack directly over medium heat for about 2 minutes or until lightly charred, turning once halfway through grilling. (For a grill pan, preheat grill pan. Place lettuce in pan and cook as directed.)

4. Place each lettuce half on a salad plate along with bacon and cherry tomatoes. Drizzle with salad dressing and, if desired, top with cheese.

*TIP To make ¼ cup sour milk, place 1 teaspoon lemon juice or vinegar in a glass measuring cup. Add enough milk to equal ¼ cup total liquid; stir. Let stand for 5 minutes before using. To make ½ cup sour milk, place 2 teaspoons lemon juice or vinegar in a glass measuring cup. Add enough milk to equal ½ cup total liquid; stir. Let stand for 5 minutes before using.

PER SERVING *223 cal., 19 g fat (7 g sat. fat), 32 mg chol., 516 mg sodium, 4 g carb., 1 g fiber, 9 g pro.*

PREP **15 minutes**
BAKE **15 minutes at 375°F**
GRILL **2 minutes**

4 servings	ingredients	8 servings
2 Tbsp.	crème fraîche or sour cream	¼ cup
2 Tbsp.	mayonnaise or salad dressing	¼ cup
1 Tbsp.	snipped fresh dill	2 Tbsp.
1 Tbsp.	apple cider vinegar	2 Tbsp.
1	clove garlic, minced	2
¼ cup	buttermilk or sour milk*	½ cup
	Salt and freshly ground black pepper	
4	slices bacon	8
2	heads romaine lettuce	4
	Olive oil	
1 cup	cherry tomatoes, halved	2 cups
½ cup (2 oz.)	shaved Parmesan cheese (optional)	1 cup (4 oz.)

Harvest Slaw

Perfect with roast pork or pork chops, this red cabbage-and-apple slaw provides gorgeous color and a fresh crunch to an autumnal meal.

1. For dressing, in a large skillet heat olive oil over medium heat. Add garlic and caraway seeds; cook and stir for 1 minute. Whisk in vinegar and honey; bring to a simmer. Season with the salt and pepper.

2. In a large bowl toss together the cabbage, apple, cranberries, and pecans. Add dressing and toss to combine. Top with cilantro.

PER SERVING *105 cal., 7 g fat (1 g sat. fat), 0 chol., 56 mg sodium, 13 g carb., 2 g fiber, 1 g pro.*

START TO FINISH **30 minutes**

6 servings	ingredients	12 servings
4 tsp.	olive oil	3 Tbsp.
1	cloves garlic, coarsely chopped	2
1 tsp.	caraway seeds, lightly crushed	2 tsp.
2 Tbsp.	cider vinegar	¼ cup
1½ tsp.	honey	1 Tbsp.
⅛ tsp.	salt	¼ tsp.
⅛ tsp.	black pepper	¼ tsp.
2 cups	finely shredded red cabbage (or red and green)	4 cups
1	red apple, cored and thinly sliced	2
¼ cup	dried cranberries	½ cup
¼ cup	pecan halves, toasted (see tip, page 28)	½ cup
1 Tbsp.	fresh cilantro or parsley leaves	2 Tbsp.

Desserts

Satisfy your sweet tooth with this selection of brownies, bars, cakes, cookies, cobblers, and crisps. You'll find just the right treat for any occasion.

168

177

187

Apricot Coffee Cake

PREP 25 minutes
BAKE 35 minutes at 350°F

6 servings	ingredients	12 servings
¾ cup + 2 Tbsp.	all-purpose flour	1¾ cups
½ tsp.	baking powder	1 tsp.
¼ tsp.	baking soda	½ tsp.
⅛ tsp.	salt	¼ tsp.
¼ cup	butter, softened	½ cup
½	8-oz. pkg. cream cheese, softened	1
½ cup + 2 Tbsp.	granulated sugar	1¼ cups
1	egg, slightly beaten	2
½ tsp.	almond extract or vanilla	1 tsp.
2 Tbsp.	milk	¼ cup
¼ cup	all-purpose flour	½ cup
¼ cup	packed brown sugar	½ cup
1 tsp.	ground cinnamon	2 tsp.
2 Tbsp.	butter	¼ cup
¼ cup	chopped walnuts or almonds	½ cup
½	24- to 26-oz. jar apricot halves, drained and cut in half	1

Apricots and almond are natural partners. In this homey cake, an almond-flavored cream-cheese cake is topped with a buttery crumb topping and juicy, sweet-tart apricot halves.

1. Preheat oven to 350°F. Grease and flour an 8×8×2-inch baking pan; set aside. In a medium bowl combine the ¾ cup plus 2 tablespoons flour, baking powder, baking soda, and salt; set aside.

2. In a large mixing bowl beat ¼ cup butter and cream cheese with an electric mixer on medium for 30 seconds. Add granulated sugar. Beat on medium to high until light and fluffy. Add egg and almond extract; beat well. Alternately add flour mixture and milk to beaten egg mixture, beating until smooth after each addition.

3. Spread batter into prepared pan. Bake for 25 to 30 minutes or until top is lightly browned. Meanwhile, in a small bowl combine the ¼ cup all-purpose flour, brown sugar, and ground cinnamon. Cut in butter until mixture resembles coarse crumbs. Stir in walnuts; set aside. Carefully arrange apricots on cake. Sprinkle nut mixture over cake.

4. Bake for 10 to 15 minutes more or until a toothpick inserted near the center comes out clean. Serve warm.

FOR 12 SERVINGS Prepare using method above, except in Step 1 use a 13×9×2-inch baking pan and the 1¾ cups flour. In Step 2 use ½ cup butter. In Step 3 use the ½ cup flour.

PER SERVING *445 cal., 22 g fat (12 g sat. fat), 87 mg chol., 279 mg sodium, 57 g carb., 2 g fiber, 4 g pro.*

Sour Cream-Orange Coffee Cake with Chocolate Streusel

The indulgent topping and streusel ribbon through the center of the cake is the same fabulous mixture—brown sugar, flour, cocoa powder, butter, chocolate pieces, and pecans.

1. Preheat oven to 350°F. Grease an 8×8×2-inch baking pan; set aside. For chocolate streusel, in a bowl stir together brown sugar, the ¼ cup flour, and the cocoa powder. Using a pastry blender, cut in the cold butter until mixture resembles coarse crumbs. Stir in chocolate pieces and pecans; set aside.

2. In a medium bowl stir together the flour, baking powder, baking soda, and salt. Mix orange peel into flour mixture. Set aside.

3. In an extra-large mixing bowl beat the ⅓ cup softened butter and granulated sugar with an electric mixer on medium for 2 minutes. Add egg, beating well. Beat in sour cream, milk, orange juice, and vanilla until combined. Gradually beat in flour mixture on low. Beat about 2 minutes or until smooth.

4. Spread half the batter in the prepared pan. Evenly sprinkle half of the streusel over the batter. Using the back of a spoon, gently press streusel into batter. Spread remaining batter over streusel. Sprinkle with remaining streusel.

5. Bake for 50 to 55 minutes or until a wooden toothpick inserted near center comes out clean. Cool in pan on a wire rack at least 15 minutes. Serve warm.

FOR 24 SERVINGS Prepare using method above, except in Step 1 use a 13×9×2-inch baking pan. Use ½ cup flour. In Step 2 use 3¾ cups flour. In Step 4 use ¾ cup softened butter.

PER SERVING *317 cal., 14 g fat (8 g sat. fat), 44 mg chol., 243 mg sodium, 45 g carb., 1 g fiber, 4 g pro.*

PREP **20 minutes**
BAKE **50 minutes at 350°F**
COOL **15 minutes**

12 servings	ingredients	24 servings
¼ cup	packed brown sugar	½ cup
¼ cup	all-purpose flour	½ cup
1½ tsp.	unsweetened cocoa powder	1 Tbsp.
2 Tbsp.	cold butter, cut up	¼ cup
⅓ cup	miniature semisweet chocolate pieces	¾ cup
¼ cup	chopped pecans	½ cup
1¾ cups + 2 Tbsp.	all-purpose flour	3¾ cups
½ Tbsp.	baking powder	1 Tbsp.
½ tsp.	baking soda	1 tsp.
¼ tsp. + ⅛ tsp.	salt	¾ tsp.
1 tsp.	finely shredded orange peel	2 tsp.
⅓ cup	butter, softened	¾ cup
1 cup	granulated sugar	2 cups
1	egg	2
½	8-oz. carton sour cream	1
⅓ cup	milk	¾ cup
2 Tbsp.	orange juice	¼ cup
¾ tsp.	vanilla	1½ tsp.

Peanut Butter Jammin' Bars

The flavors of a favorite sandwich get fancied up in these PB&J bars. Use any kind of jam you like—blackberry, raspberry, or strawberry.

1. Preheat oven to 375°F. Line an 8×8×2-inch baking pan with foil, extending foil beyond edges of pan. Lightly grease the foil; set pan aside.

2. For crust, in a large mixing bowl beat butter and peanut butter with an electric mixer on medium to high for 30 seconds. Beat in brown sugar, vanilla, baking soda, and salt until combined, scraping sides of bowl occasionally. Beat in the oats and as much of the flour as you can with the mixer. Stir in any remaining flour (mixture will be crumbly). Reserve 1 cup of the oat mixture. Firmly press remaining oat mixture into the bottom of the prepared pan; set aside.

3. In a small bowl whisk the jam until smooth; evenly spread jam over the crust to within 1 inch of edges. Evenly sprinkle with the reserved oat mixture and the chocolate-covered peanuts.

4. Bake for 25 to 30 minutes or until jam is bubbly and topping is golden brown. Cool completely in pan on a wire rack. Use foil to lift uncut bars out of the pan. Transfer to a cutting board. Cut into bars.

FOR 32 SERVINGS Prepare using method above, except in Step 1 use a 13×9×2-inch baking pan. In Step 2 use an extra-large mixing bowl and reserve 2 cups of the oat mixture.

PER SERVING *213 cal., 9 g fat (4 g sat. fat), 12 mg chol., 121 mg sodium, 32 g carb., 2 g fiber, 3 g pro.*

PREP **20 minutes**
BAKE **25 minutes at 375°F**

16 servings	ingredients	32 servings
⅓ cup	butter, softened	¾ cup
¼ cup	creamy peanut butter	½ cup
¾ cup	packed brown sugar	1½ cups
½ tsp.	vanilla	1 tsp.
¼ tsp.	baking soda	½ tsp.
¼ tsp.	salt	½ tsp.
1 cup + 2 Tbsp.	quick-cooking rolled oats	2¼ cups
1 cup	all-purpose flour	2 cups
½	12-oz. jar seedless blackberry, raspberry, or strawberry jam	1
½ cup	chocolate-covered peanuts, coarsely chopped	1 cup

No-Bake Coconut-Date Cracker Bars with Browned Butter Glaze

PREP 30 minutes
COOK 8 minutes
CHILL 2 hours

24 servings	ingredients	48 servings
36	rich rectangular crackers	72
¾ cup	packed brown sugar	1½ cup
½ cup	whipping cream	1 cup
⅓ cup	butter	⅔ cup
2	egg yolks	4
½ tsp.	salt	1 tsp.
1 cup	flaked coconut	2 cups
1 cup	chopped pitted dates	2 cups
¾ cup	chopped pecans or walnuts	1½ cups
1 Tbsp.	dark rum	2 Tbsp.
1 tsp.	vanilla	2 tsp.
¼ cup	butter	½ cup
1 cup	powdered sugar	2 cups
1 Tbsp.	milk	2 Tbsp.
⅛ tsp.	salt	¼ tsp.
⅓ cup	chopped pecans or walnuts	⅔ cup

These chewy and decadent bars are fine enough to take to a party—and you don't even have to turn your oven on to make them.

1. Line an 8×8×2-inch baking pan with foil, extending foil beyond the edges of pan. Lightly butter foil. Arrange half of the crackers in a single layer to completely cover the bottom of pan, cutting some to fit if necessary. Set aside.

2. For filling, in a medium saucepan combine brown sugar, cream, the ⅓ cup butter, egg yolks, and ½ teaspoon salt. Melt butter, stirring constantly. Stir in coconut, dates, and the ¾ cup pecans. Cook for 8 minutes, stirring constantly, or until filling is glossy and a rich shade of brown. Remove from heat. Stir in rum and vanilla.

3. Pour filling over the cracker layer, spreading gently to completely cover crackers. Arrange the remaining crackers over the filling, pressing lightly into the filling. Set aside.

4. For the glaze, in a small saucepan melt the ¼ cup butter over medium heat; cook until butter is light brown. Transfer to a small bowl. Whisk in the powdered sugar, milk, and ⅛ teaspoon salt until smooth, adding additional milk as necessary for a spreadable glaze. Pour the glaze over the top, spreading evenly. Sprinkle with the ⅓ cup pecans. Cover and chill about 2 hours or until set.

5. Use foil to lift uncut bars out of pan. Transfer to a cutting board. Using a serrated knife, cut into bars.

FOR 48 SERVINGS Prepare using method above, except in Step 1 use a 13×9×2-inch baking pan. In Step 2 use ⅔ cup butter, 1 teaspoon salt, and 1½ cups pecans. In Step 4 use ½ cup butter, ¼ teaspoon salt, and ⅔ cup pecans.

PER SERVING *205 cal., 12 g fat (5 g sat. fat), 34 mg chol., 161 mg sodium, 23 g carb., 2 g fiber, 1 g pro.*

Chocolate-Drizzled Caramel-Hazelnut Bars

With caramel, nuts, and chocolate, these rich bars are more confection than cookie.

1. Preheat oven to 350°F. Line an 8×8×2-inch baking pan with heavy foil, extending foil beyond edges of pan. Lightly coat foil with cooking spray; set pan aside.

2. For crust, in a food processor combine flour, powdered sugar, and ⅓ cup + 2 tablespoons cold butter. Cover and pulse until mixture forms coarse crumbs. Press firmly and evenly into the bottom and ¾ inch up the sides of the prepared pan. Bake for 18 to 20 minutes or until edges begin to brown. Transfer pan to a wire rack to cool for 20 minutes.

3. For filling, in a medium saucepan combine brown sugar, honey, the ⅓ cup butter, and whipping cream. Cook and stir over medium heat until mixture boils. Stir in toasted hazelnuts. Spoon nut mixture on the partially baked crust. Bake for 20 to 25 minutes or until filling is golden and bubbly. Transfer pan to a wire rack; cool completely.

4. Use foil to lift uncut bars out of pan. Place on a cutting board. Using a sharp knife, trim edges. Cut into bars.

5. In a small saucepan combine chocolate pieces and shortening. Stir over low heat until melted and smooth. Drizzle over bars; let stand until chocolate is set.

FOR 36 SERVINGS Prepare using method above, except in Step 1 use a 13×9×2-inch baking pan. In Step 2 use ¾ cup cold butter. In Step 3 use the ⅔ cup butter.

PER SERVING 227 cal., 17 g fat (6 g sat. fat), 21 mg chol., 66 mg sodium, 19 g carb., 2 g fiber, 3 g pro.

PREP 45 minutes
BAKE 40 minutes at 350°F
COOL 50 minutes

18 servings	ingredients	36 servings
	Nonstick cooking spray	
1 cups	all-purpose flour	2 cups
⅓ cup	powdered sugar	⅔ cup
⅓ cup + 2 Tbsp.	cold butter, cut up	¾ cup
¼ cup	packed brown sugar	½ cup
¼ cup	honey	½ cup
⅓ cup	butter	⅔ cup
4 tsp.	whipping cream	3 Tbsp.
⅓ cup + 2 Tbsp.	semisweet chocolate pieces	¾ cup
1 tsp.	shortening	2 tsp.
1¾ cups	hazelnuts, toasted (see tip, page 67)	3½ cups

Blueberry Swirl Cheesecake Bars

When you don't want an entire wedge of cheesecake, these blueberry-studded bars provide just a bite or two of that rich, silky goodness.

PREP 25 minutes
BAKE 40 minutes at 350°F
COOL 1 hour
CHILL 1 hour

18 servings	ingredients	36 servings
1 Tbsp.	granulated sugar	2 Tbsp.
1 tsp.	cornstarch	2 tsp.
½ cup	fresh or frozen blueberries	1 cup
2 Tbsp.	orange juice	¼ cup
1 cup	all-purpose flour	2 cups
¼ cup	powdered sugar	½ cup
½ cup	butter	1 cup
½	8-oz. pkg. cream cheese, softened	1
¼ cup	granulated sugar	½ cup
1½ tsp.	all-purpose flour	1 Tbsp.
1	egg, lightly beaten	2
½ tsp.	vanilla	1 tsp.
	Powdered sugar (optional)	

1. Preheat oven to 350°F. Line an 8×8×2-inch baking pan with foil, extending foil beyond edges of pan; set baking pan aside.

2. In a small saucepan stir together the 1 tablespoon sugar and cornstarch. Stir in blueberries and orange juice. Cook and stir over medium heat until thickened and bubbly. Remove from heat and set aside.

3. For crust, in a large bowl stir together 1 cup flour and ¼ cup powdered sugar. Cut in butter until fine crumbs form and mixture starts to cling together (mixture will still be crumbly). Pat firmly into prepared pan. Bake for 20 minutes.

4. Meanwhile, for filling, in a medium bowl beat cream cheese, ¼ cup sugar and 1½ teaspoons flour until smooth. Beat in eggs and vanilla until combined. Pour over hot baked crust, spreading evenly. Spoon blueberry mixture in small mounds over filling. Use a thin metal spatula or table knife to swirl.

5. Bake for 20 minutes or until center is set. Remove and cool in pan on a wire rack for 1 hour. Cover and chill at least 1 hour. Lift uncut bars from pan with foil. Cut into bars. If desired, sift with powdered sugar just before serving.

FOR 36 SERVINGS Prepare using method above, except in Step 1 use a 13×9×2-inch baking pan. In Step 2 use a medium saucepan and 2 tablespoons sugar. In Step 3 use 2 cups flour. In Step 4 use ½ cup sugar and 1 tablespoon flour.

PER SERVING *120 cal., 8 g fat (5 g sat. fat), 32 mg chol., 61 mg sodium, 12 g carb., 0 g fiber, 2 g pro.*

Chocolate-Raspberry Cheesecake Bars

Chocolate pairs with certain fruits to varying degrees. It is particularly nice with orange and cherry—and it goes spectacularly well with sweet-tart raspberries.

PREP 30 minutes
BAKE 25 minutes at 350°F
CHILL 1 hour

16 servings	ingredients	32 servings
1 cup (20 cookies)	crushed chocolate wafer cookies	2 cups (40 cookies)
3 Tbsp.	butter, melted	6 Tbsp.
½	8-oz. pkg. cream cheese, softened	1
⅓ cup	sour cream	⅔ cup
¼ cup	sugar	½ cup
1	egg	2
1 Tbsp.	raspberry liqueur (optional)	2 Tbsp.
1 tsp.	cornstarch	2 tsp.
½ tsp.	finely shredded lemon peel	1 tsp.
1 cup	fresh raspberries	2 cups
	Seedless raspberry jam or currant jelly, melted (optional)	

1. Preheat oven to 350°F. Line an 8×8×2-inch baking pan with foil, extending foil beyond edges of pan. Lightly grease foil. For crust, in a small bowl stir together crushed wafers and melted butter. Pat crumb mixture firmly into the bottom of prepared pan; set aside.

2. For filling, in a medium mixing bowl beat cream cheese with an electric mixer on medium to high until smooth. Add sour cream and sugar. Beat until combined, scraping sides of bowl occasionally. Beat in egg just until combined. Add raspberry liqueur (if using), cornstarch, and lemon peel. Beat on low just until combined. Pour the filling over the crust in pan, spreading evenly. Arrange raspberries on filling.

3. Bake for 25 to 30 minutes or until center is set. Cool in pan on a wire rack. Cover and chill for at least 1 hour or overnight.

FOR 32 SERVINGS Prepare using method above, except in Step 1 use a 13×9×2-inch baking pan.

PER SERVING *106 cal., 7 g fat (4 g sat. fat), 27 mg chol., 101 mg sodium, 10 g carb., 1 g fiber, 2 g pro.*

Four-Layer Caramel Crunch Nougat Brownies

These striped goodies feature four irresistible layers—brownie, caramel and crisp rice cereal, peanut butter and marshmallow nougat, and chocolate ganache.

1. In a saucepan melt unsweetened chocolate and ¼ cup butter over low heat until smooth; cool slightly. Preheat oven to 350°F. Grease an 8×8×2-inch baking pan.

2. For brownie layer, stir ½ cup of the sugar into chocolate. Add eggs, one at a time, beating just until combined. Stir in vanilla, flour, and baking soda; spread in baking pan. Bake for 15 to 17 minutes or until edges start to pull away from sides of pan. Cool on a wire rack.

3. For caramel layer, in a microwave-safe bowl mix caramels, 1 tablespoon of the milk, and water. Heat on high for 2½ minutes or until caramels are melted, stirring every 30 seconds. Stir in cereal. Spread caramel over brownie layer. Freeze while preparing nougat layer.

4. For nougat layer, in a saucepan mix remaining sugar, remaining milk, and the 3 tablespoons butter. Bring to boiling over medium-high, stirring constantly; reduce to medium. Boil at a moderate, steady rate, without stirring, for 10 minutes; remove from heat. Place marshmallow creme and peanut butter in a heatproof bowl. Whisk in marshmallow creme and peanut butter. Pour nougat over caramel layer. Freeze while preparing chocolate layer.

5. For chocolate layer, in a saucepan melt semisweet chocolate pieces, whipping cream, and 4½ teaspoons butter over low heat. Pour over nougat layer. Cover; chill for 2 hours. Cut into bars.

FOR 64 SERVINGS Prepare using method above, except in Step 1 use ½ cup butter and a 13×9×2-inch baking pan. In Step 2 use 1 cup of the sugar. In Step 3 use 2 tablespoons milk. In Step 4 use ⅓ cup butter. In Step 5 use 3 tablespoons butter.

PER SERVING *158 cal., 8 g fat (5 g sat. fat), 28 mg chol., 82 mg sodium, 21 g carb., 1 g fiber, 2 g pro.*

PREP **50 minutes**
BAKE **15 minutes at 350°F**
CHILL **2 hours**

32 servings	ingredients	64 servings
1½ oz.	unsweetened chocolate, coarsely chopped	3 oz.
¼ cup	butter	½ cup
1 cup + 2 Tbsp.	sugar	2¼ cup
1	eggs	2
½ tsp.	vanilla	1 tsp.
⅓ cup	all-purpose flour	⅔ cup
⅛ tsp.	baking soda	¼ tsp.
32	vanilla caramels, unwrapped	68
⅓ cup	evaporated milk	⅔ cup
1½ tsp.	water	1 Tbsp.
¾ cup	crisp rice cereal	1½ cups
3 Tbsp.	butter	⅓ cup
½	7 oz. jar marshmallow creme	1
2 Tbsp.	creamy peanut butter	¼ cup
1 cup	semisweet chocolate pieces	2 cups
3 Tbsp.	whipping cream	⅓ cup
4½ tsp.	butter	3 Tbsp.

16 servings	ingredients	32 servings
1 cup	all-purpose flour	2 cups
1¼ tsp.	baking powder	2½ tsp.
¼ tsp.	salt	½ tsp.
1 cup	packed brown sugar	2 cups
⅓ cup	butter, softened	¾ cup
½ tsp.	vanilla	1 tsp.
2	eggs	3
½ cup	tiny marshmallows	1 cup
½ cup	chopped unsalted cashews or toffee pieces	1 cup
½	11.5- to 12-oz. pkg. bittersweet chocolate or white baking pieces	1

Blondie Stix

These chocolate-dipped blondies speckled with itty-bitty marshmallows and stuck on a stick make whimsical and fun party treats.

1. Preheat oven to 350°F. Line an 8×8×2-inch baking pan with foil, extending foil beyond narrow edges of pan. Grease foil; set pan aside.

2. In a small bowl combine flour, baking powder, and salt; set aside. In a large mixing bowl combine brown sugar, butter, and vanilla. Beat with an electric mixer on medium-high until combined. Beat in eggs, one at a time, beating well after each. Gradually beat in flour mixture. Stir in marshmallows. Spread batter in prepared pan.

3. Bake about 30 minutes or until top is golden and edges are firm. Cool on a wire rack. Using edges of foil, lift uncut brownies out of pan. Invert onto a cutting board; remove foil. Trim away edges to a 12×8-inch rectangle. Cut rectangle into sixteen 3×1-inch bars. Cover and freeze about 30 minutes or until firm.

4. Insert a 6- to 8-inch wooden stick into each brownie; place on a waxed paper-lined baking sheet. Place cashews in a small shallow bowl. In a small saucepan melt chocolate pieces over low heat.

5. Dip half of each brownie into melted chocolate, allowing excess to drip back into saucepan. Immediately sprinkle with cashews. Place on prepared baking sheet. Let stand about 1 hour or until chocolate is set.

FOR 36 SERVINGS Prepare using method above, except in Step 1 use a 13×9×2-inch baking pan. In Step 3 cut 32 bars.

PER SERVING *211 cal., 11 g fat (6 g sat. fat), 32 mg chol., 109 mg sodium, 28 g carb., 1 g fiber, 3 g pro.*

Almond-Apricot Blondies

Some people have a reaction to the sulfur used to keep apricots pliable and bright in color when dried. If you have this issue, look for unsulfured dried apricots at a health food store. They will be slightly harder and darker in color, but their flavor will be fine.

1. In a small saucepan combine dried apricots and amaretto. Bring just to boiling; cool. Preheat oven to 350°F. Line an 8×8×2-inch baking pan with foil, extending foil beyond edges of pan. Lightly grease foil; set pan aside.

2. In a medium saucepan melt and stir brown sugar and butter over medium heat until smooth; cool slightly. Add eggs, one at a time, beating with a wooden spoon just until combined. Stir in vanilla. Stir in flour, baking powder, baking soda, and salt until combined. Stir in undrained apricots. Fold in ¾ cup of the almonds. Evenly spread batter in prepared pan.

3. Bake about 35 minutes or until a wooden toothpick inserted near center comes out clean. Cool slightly in pan on a wire rack.

4. Meanwhile, in a small saucepan bring apricot preserves to boiling over medium-high heat. Reduce heat to medium-low; simmer, uncovered, about 10 minutes or until slightly thickened. Cool for 5 minutes.

5. Gently spread preserves over warm uncut bars. Sprinkle with remaining almonds. Using edges of foil, lift uncut bars out of pan. Cut into bars.

FOR 32 SERVINGS Prepare using method above, except in Step 1 use a 13×9×2-inch baking pan. In Step 2 fold in 1½ cups of the almonds.

PER SERVING *198 cal., 7 g fat (3 g sat. fat), 22 mg chol., 89 mg sodium, 31 g carb., 1 g fiber, 3 g pro.*

PREP 30 minutes
BAKE 35 minutes at 350°F

16 servings	ingredients	32 servings
½ cup	dried apricots, coarsely snipped	1 cup
2 Tbsp.	amaretto or apricot nectar	¼ cup
1 cup	packed brown sugar	2 cups
⅓ cup	butter	⅔ cup
1	egg	2
1 tsp.	vanilla	2 tsp.
1 cup	all-purpose flour	2 cups
½ tsp.	baking powder	1 tsp.
⅛ tsp.	baking soda	¼ tsp.
⅛ tsp.	salt	¼ tsp.
1 cup	sliced almonds, toasted (see tip, page 28)	2 cups
½ cup	apricot preserves	1 cup

Macadamia Shortbread

Two tropical treats—coconut and macadamia nuts—give this shortbread flavor and texture.

1. Preheat oven to 350°F. Line a large cookie sheet with parchment paper; set aside.

2. In a large mixing bowl beat butter with an electric mixer on medium to high for 30 seconds. Add sugar and vanilla. Beat until combined, scraping sides of bowl occasionally. Add flour, salt, ground macadamia nuts, and coconut; beat on low until dough comes together. Divide dough in half.

3. Place balls on the prepared cookie sheet. Pat or roll balls into 7-inch circles. Using a sharp knife or pizza cutter, cut each circle into 12 wedges. Press a macadamia nut half onto the wide end of each wedge. Leave wedges in the circles.

4. Bake about 25 minutes or until edges are light brown and centers are set. Recut circles into wedges while warm. Cool on cookie sheet for 10 minutes. Transfer to a wire rack; cool.

FOR 48 SERVINGS Prepare using method above, except in Step 1 use two large cookie sheets. In Step 2 divide dough in fourths.

PER SERVING *186 cal., 13 g fat (6 g sat. fat), 20 mg chol., 93 mg sodium, 15 g carb., 1 g fiber, 2 g pro.*

PREP **20 minutes**
BAKE **25 minutes at 350°F**
COOL **10 minutes**

24 servings	ingredients	48 servings
1 cup	butter, softened	2 cups
½ cup	sugar	1 cup
1 Tbsp.	vanilla	2 Tbsp.
2½ cups	all-purpose flour	5 cups
¼ tsp.	salt	½ tsp.
¾ cup	ground macadamia nuts	1½ cups
¼ cup	shredded coconut, toasted (see tip, page 28)	½ cup
24	macadamia nut halves	48

Triple-Peanut and Chocolate Chip Cookies

The peanut butter cup crowns and honey-sweetened peanuts turn ordinary chocolate chip cookies into royal treats .

1. Preheat oven to 350°F. In a large mixing bowl beat butter, shortening, and peanut butter with an electric mixer on medium to high for 30 seconds. Add the brown sugar, granulated sugar, and baking soda. Beat until combined, scraping sides of bowl occasionally. Beat in egg and vanilla until combined. Beat in as much of the flour as you can with the mixer. Stir in any remaining flour, chocolate pieces, and peanuts.

2. Drop dough by rounded teaspoons 2 inches apart onto ungreased cookie sheets. Press a peanut butter cup into each cookie. Bake for 10 to 12 minutes or until golden brown. Transfer to a wire rack and let cool.

PER SERVING *97 cal., 5 g fat (2 g sat. fat), 9 mg chol., 47 mg sodium, 11 g carb., 2 g pro.*

PREP 25 minutes
BAKE 10 minutes at 350°F

36 servings	ingredients	72 servings
¼ cup	butter, softened	½ cup
¼ cup	shortening	½ cup
¼ cup	creamy peanut butter	½ cup
½ cup	packed brown sugar	1 cup
¼ cup	granulated sugar	½ cup
½ tsp.	baking soda	1 tsp.
1	eggs	2
½ tsp.	vanilla	1 tsp.
1½ cups	all-purpose flour	3 cups
36	bite-size miniature chocolate-covered peanut butter cups	72
¼ cup	semisweet chocolate pieces	½ cup
¼ cup	milk chocolate pieces	½ cup
¼ cup	honey-roasted peanuts	½ cup

Peanut Butter, Jelly, and Brownie Cookies

PREP 25 minutes
FREEZE 30 minutes
BAKE 30 minutes at 350°F

16 servings	ingredients	32 servings
1	16.5-oz. pkg. refrigerated peanut butter cookie dough	2
¾ cup	butter	1½ cups
3 oz.	unsweetened chocolate, coarsely chopped	6 oz.
1⅓ cups	sugar	2⅔ cups
2 tsp.	vanilla	4 tsp.
3	eggs	6
1 cup	all-purpose flour	2 cups
2 Tbsp.	unsweetened cocoa powder	¼ cup
⅓ cup	strawberry or cherry jam, jelly, or preserves	⅔ cup

It's been well established that peanut butter and jelly go great together—and so do peanut butter and chocolate. Now, a new discovery: The sum is greater than the parts—all three of them!

1. Preheat oven according to cookie package directions. On a lightly floured surface, use hands to slightly flatten cookie dough to an 8×2½-inch log. Place on baking sheet; freeze for 30 minutes. Slice dough in half lengthwise, then slice each half in 16 slices. Place slices on cookie sheets. Using a fork dipped in granulated sugar, make a crisscross pattern on each cookie. Bake cookies according to package directions or until golden brown. Cool on wire racks.

2. Meanwhile, for brownies, in a medium saucepan stir butter and chocolate over low heat just until melted. Remove from heat. Using a wooden spoon, stir in sugar and vanilla. Cool 5 minutes.

3. Set oven to 350°F. Line the bottom and sides of an 8×8×2-inch baking pan with heavy foil, extending foil beyond pan edges. Grease foil; set pan aside.

4. Add eggs, one at a time, to butter-chocolate mixture, beating after each just until combined. Stir in flour and cocoa powder. Evenly spread batter in prepared pan.

5. Bake for 30 to 35 minutes, just until a wooden toothpick inserted near center comes out clean. Transfer to a wire rack. Leave oven set to 350°F to warm sandwich cookies.

6. For sandwich cookies, scoop and mash warm brownie onto the flat side of a cookie. Top with 1 teaspoon jam and a second cookie. Place sandwich cookies that will be served immediately on a cookie sheet and warm in oven about 4 minutes.

FOR 32 SERVINGS Prepare using method above, except in Step 3 use a 13×9×2-inch baking pan.

PER SERVING *223 cal., 11 g fat (4 g sat. fat), 27 mg chol., 149 mg sodium, 28 g carb., 1 g fiber, 3 g pro.*

Cherry Surprise Crinkles

The surprise inside these cherry-studded cookies is a Kiss candy. You can use the cordial-filled variety or just plain chocolate.

1. Preheat oven to 350°F. In a medium mixing bowl beat butter with an electric mixer on medium to high for 30 seconds. Add the granulated sugar, baking powder, baking soda, and salt. Beat until combined, scraping sides of bowl occasionally. Beat in egg and almond extract until combined. Beat in as much of the flour as you can with the mixer. Stir in any remaining flour and the cherries.

2. Divide dough into 36 equal portions.* Shape each portion into a ball around a Kiss. Place balls 2 inches apart on ungreased cookie sheets.

3. Bake for 10 to 12 minutes or until bottoms are light golden brown. Transfer cookies to a wire rack and let cool. Lightly dust cooled cookies with powdered sugar.

*TIP To divide the dough equally, pat dough into a rectangle on a lightly floured surface. Using a sharp knife, cut the dough into 6 equal rows then cut rows, into 6 equal portions.

FOR 72 SERVINGS Prepare using method above, except in Step 2 divide dough in half, then divide each half in 36 portions. Bake half the cookies at a time.

PER SERVING *97 cal., 4 g fat (3 g sat. fat), 12 mg chol., 56 mg sodium, 15 g carb., 1 g fiber, 1 g pro.*

PREP 30 minutes
BAKE 10 minutes at 350°F

36 servings	ingredients	72 servings
½ cup	butter, softened	1 cup
1 cup	granulated sugar	2 cups
½ tsp.	baking powder	1 tsp.
¼ tsp.	baking soda	½ tsp.
¼ tsp.	salt	½ tsp.
1	egg	2
1 tsp.	almond extract	2 tsp.
2 cups	all-purpose flour	4 cups
½ cup	chopped maraschino cherries, well drained and patted dry with paper toweling	1 cup
36	Kisses cherry cordials or Kisses dark chocolates	72
	Powdered sugar	

Coconut Macaroons

Chopped macadamia nuts add texture and an element of buttery richness to this classic cookie.

1. Preheat oven to 325°F. Line a large cookie sheet with parchment paper; set aside.

2. In a large bowl combine coconut, macadamia nuts, sugar, flour, and salt. Add egg whites, lemon peel, and lemon juice, stirring until combined. Drop dough by rounded teaspoons 2 inches apart onto the prepared cookie sheet.

3. Bake for 20 to 25 minutes or until edges are lightly browned. Transfer cookies to a wire rack; cool. If desired, sprinkle with powdered sugar.

FOR 60 SERVINGS Prepare using method above, except in Step 1 use two cookie sheets.

PER SERVING *85 cal., 5 g fat (3 g sat. fat), 0 g chol., 55 mg sodium, 9 g carb., 1 g fiber, 1 g pro.*

PREP 25 minutes
BAKE 20 minutes at 325°F

30 servings	ingredients	60 servings
2 cups	flaked coconut	4 cups
¾ cup	coarsely chopped macadamia nuts	1½ cups
⅔ cup	sugar	1⅓ cups
⅓ cup	all-purpose flour	⅔ cup
¼ tsp.	salt	½ tsp.
3	egg whites, lightly beaten	6
1 tsp.	finely shredded lemon peel	2 tsp.
1 Tbsp.	lemon juice	2 Tbsp.
	Powdered sugar (optional)	

Strawberry-Chocolate Turnovers

These taste (and look) like they came from a fancy French bakery. Thanks to frozen puff pastry, they are a cinch to make.

1. Preheat oven to 400°F. Line a large baking sheet with parchment paper; set aside.

2. Unfold puff pastry sheets. On a lightly floured surface, roll each sheet of puff pastry into a 12-inch square. Cut each square into nine 4-inch squares (18 squares total). Spoon 1 teaspoon mascarpone cheese onto center of each pastry square. Top each with 1 teaspoon strawberry jam and 1 tablespoon chopped chocolate. Brush the edges of the squares with egg. Fold squares in half diagonally to enclose the filling; press edges together with the tines of a fork to seal.

3. Place triangles 2 inches apart on the prepared baking sheet. Prick tops of triangles with a fork. Brush tops with egg; sprinkle with sliced almonds and coarse sugar.

4. Bake for 16 to 20 minutes or until puffed and golden brown. Transfer to a wire rack; cool slightly. If desired, drizzle with melted chocolate.

FOR 36 SERVINGS Prepare using method above, except in Step 1 line two baking sheets. In Step 2 cut 36 squares total.

PER SERVING *198 cal., 13 g fat (2 g sat. fat), 17 mg chol., 115 mg sodium, 19 g carb., 1 g fiber, 3 g pro.*

PREP **30 minutes**
BAKE **16 minutes at 400°F**

18 servings	ingredients	36 servings
1 (2 sheets)	17.3-oz. pkg. frozen puff pastry sheets, thawed	2 (4 sheets)
⅓ cup	mascarpone cheese or cream cheese, softened	⅔ cup
⅓ cup	strawberry jam	⅔ cup
4 oz.	milk chocolate, chopped	8 oz.
1	egg, lightly beaten	2
2 Tbsp.	sliced almonds	¼ cup
	Coarse sugar	
2 oz.	milk chocolate, melted (optional)	4 oz.

Strawberry-Rhubarb Crisp

PREP 15 minutes
BAKE 40 minutes at 375°F
COOL 20 minutes

6 servings	ingredients	12 servings
⅓ cup	strawberry preserves	⅔ cup
⅛ tsp.	ground cinnamon or nutmeg	¼ tsp.
2 cups	sliced fresh strawberries	4 cups
2 cups	sliced fresh rhubarb	4 cups
3 Tbsp.	all-purpose flour	6 Tbsp.
½ cup	quick-cooking rolled oats	1 cup
2 Tbsp.	cornmeal	¼ cup
2 Tbsp.	honey	¼ cup
1 tsp.	vanilla	2 tsp.

Late spring, when both strawberries and rhubarb are in season, presents a sweet but fleeting opportunity to make this homey crisp. Serve it warm with a scoop of vanilla-bean ice cream.

1. Preheat oven to 375°F. In a large bowl stir together preserves and cinnamon. Add strawberries and rhubarb; stir gently to coat. Add flour; stir gently until combined. Spoon into an 8×8×2-inch baking dish. Bake, uncovered, for 20 minutes.

2. Meanwhile, for topping, in a small bowl stir together oats and cornmeal. Stir in honey and vanilla until combined. Sprinkle over hot fruit. Bake, uncovered, about 20 minutes more or until topping is golden brown and fruit is tender.

3. Cool about 20 minutes before serving. Serve warm.

FOR 12 SERVINGS Prepare using method above, except in Step 1 use an extra-large bowl and a 13×9×2-inch baking dish.

PER SERVING *145 cal., 1 g fat (0 g sat. fat), 9 mg sodium, 0 g chol., 33 g carb., 3 g fiber, 2 g pro.*

Doughnut-Apple Cobbler

Dessert doesn't get much easier to put together than this decadent doughnut cobbler. Serve it with vanilla or cinnamon ice cream.

1. Preheat oven to 375°F. Peel, core, and cut apples into wedges; halve wedges crosswise for pieces smaller than 2 inches. Juice the lemon, retaining as much pulp as possible; toss juice and pulp with apples. Sprinkle with sugar and flour; toss to coat apples. Arrange apples in a 2-quart baking dish.

2. Top apples with doughnut pieces and drizzle with melted butter. Bake about 45 minutes or until filling is bubbly, covering with foil if necessary to prevent overbrowning. Serve warm.

FOR 12 SERVINGS Prepare using method above, except in Step 1 use a 3-quart baking dish.

PER SERVING *322 cal., 12 g fat (5 g sat. fat), 13 mg chol., 216 mg sodium, 56 g carb., 5 g fiber, 3 g pro.*

PREP 45 minutes
BAKE 45 minutes at 375°F

6 servings	ingredients	12 servings
2	medium Northern Spy or Granny Smith apples	4
1	medium Rhode Island Greening or Granny Smith apple	2
1	medium Cortland apple	2
1	medium McIntosh apple	2
½	large lemon	1
¼ cup	sugar	½ cup
3 Tbsp.	all-purpose flour	⅓ cup
3	cinnamon-sugar-coated cake doughnuts, broken into pieces	6
3 tsp.	butter, melted	5 Tbsp.

Index

Metric Information

PRODUCT DIFFERENCES

Most of the ingredients called for in the recipes in this book are available in most countries. However, some are known by different names. Here are some common American ingredients and their possible counterparts:

- Sugar (white) is granulated, fine granulated, or castor sugar.
- Powdered sugar is icing sugar.
- All-purpose flour is enriched bleached, or unbleached white household flour. When self-rising flour is used in place of all-purpose flour in a recipe that calls for leavening, omit the leavening agent (baking soda or baking powder) and salt.
- Light-color corn syrup is golden syrup.
- Cornstarch is cornflour.
- Baking soda is bicarbonate of soda.
- Vanilla or vanilla extract is vanilla essence.
- Green, red, or yellow sweet peppers are capsicums or bell peppers.
- Golden raisins are sultanas.

VOLUME AND WEIGHT

The United States traditionally uses cup measures for liquid and solid ingredients. The chart (above right) shows the approximate imperial and metric equivalents. If you are accustomed to weighing solid ingredients, the following approximate equivalents will be helpful.

- 1 cup butter, castor sugar, or rice = 8 ounces = ½ pound = 250 grams
- 1 cup flour = 4 ounces = ¼ pound = 125 grams
- 1 cup icing sugar = 5 ounces = 150 grams
- Canadian and U.S. volume for a cup measure is 8 fluid ounces (237 ml), but the standard metric equivalent is 250 ml.
- 1 British imperial cup is 10 fluid ounces.
- In Australia, 1 tablespoon equals 20 ml, and there are 4 teaspoons in the Australian tablespoon.
- Spoon measures are used for small amounts of ingredients. Although the size of the tablespoon varies slightly in different countries, for practical purposes and for recipes in this book, a straight substitution is all that's necessary. Measurements made using cups or spoons always should be level unless stated otherwise.

COMMON WEIGHT RANGE REPLACEMENTS

Imperial / U.S.	Metric
½ ounce	15 g
1 ounce	25 g or 30 g
4 ounces (¼ pound)	115 g or 125 g
8 ounces (½ pound)	225 g or 250 g
16 ounces (1 pound)	450 g or 500 g
1¼ pounds	625 g
1½ pounds	750 g
2 pounds or 2¼ pounds	1,000 g or 1 Kg

OVEN TEMPERATURE EQUIVALENTS

Fahrenheit Setting	Celsius Setting	Gas Setting
300°F	150°C	Gas Mark 2 (very low)
325°F	160°C	Gas Mark 3 (low)
350°F	180°C	Gas Mark 4 (moderate)
375°F	190°C	Gas Mark 5 (moderate)
400°F	200°C	Gas Mark 6 (hot)
425°F	220°C	Gas Mark 7 (hot)
450°F	230°C	Gas Mark 8 (very hot)
475°F	240°C	Gas Mark 9 (very hot)
500°F	260°C	Gas Mark 10 (extremely hot)
Broil	Broil	Grill

*Electric and gas ovens may be calibrated using celsius. However, for an electric oven, increase celsius setting 10 to 20 degrees when cooking above 160°C. For convection or forced air ovens (gas or electric), lower the temperature setting 25°F/10°C when cooking at all heat levels.

BAKING PAN SIZES

Imperial / U.S.	Metric
9×1½-inch round cake pan	22- or 23×4-cm (1.5 L)
9×1½-inch pie plate	22- or 23×4-cm (1 L)
8×8×2-inch square cake pan	20×5-cm (2 L)
9×9×2-inch square cake pan	22- or 23×4.5-cm (2.5 L)
11×7×1½-inch baking pan	28×17×4-cm (2 L)
2-quart rectangular baking pan	30×19×4.5-cm (3 L)
13×9×2-inch baking pan	34×22×4.5-cm (3.5 L)
15×10×1-inch jelly roll pan	40×25×2-cm
9×5×3-inch loaf pan	23×13×8-cm (2 L)
2-quart casserole	2 L

U.S./STANDARD METRIC EQUIVALENTS

⅛ teaspoon = 0.5 ml	
¼ teaspoon = 1 ml	
½ teaspoon = 2 ml	
1 teaspoon = 5 ml	
1 tablespoon = 15 ml	
2 tablespoons = 25 ml	
¼ cup = 2 fluid ounces = 50 ml	
⅓ cup = 3 fluid ounces = 75 ml	
½ cup = 4 fluid ounces = 125 ml	
⅔ cup = 5 fluid ounces = 150 ml	
¾ cup = 6 fluid ounces = 175 ml	
1 cup = 8 fluid ounces = 250 ml	
2 cups = 1 pint = 500 ml	
1 quart = 1 litre	